POWERFUL PRAYERS FOR SUPERNATURAL RESULTS

MIKE SHREVE

CHARISMA
HOUSE

Most CHARISMA HOUSE BOOK GROUP products are available at special quantity discounts for bulk purchase for sales promotions, premiums, fund-raising, and educational needs. For details, write Charisma House Book Group, 600 Rinehart Road, Lake Mary, Florida 32746, or telephone (407) 333-0600.

POWERFUL PRAYERS FOR SUPERNATURAL RESULTS
  by Mike Shreve
Published by Charisma House
Charisma Media/Charisma House Book Group
600 Rinehart Road
Lake Mary, Florida 32746
www.charismahouse.com

Unless otherwise noted, all Scripture quotations are from the New King James Version®. Copyright © 1982 by Thomas Nelson. Used by permission. All rights reserved.

Scripture quotations marked MKJV are taken from the Holy Bible, MODERN KING JAMES VERSION copyright © 1962—1998 by Jay P. Green, Sr. Used by permission of the copyright holder.

Scripture quotations marked KJV are from the King James Version of the Bible.

Cover design by Lisa Rae Cox
Design Director: Justin Evans

Visit the author's website at www.shreveministries.org.

Library of Congress Cataloging-in-Publication Data:
Shreve, Mike.
  Powerful prayers for supernatural results / Mike Shreve. -- First
edition.
      pages cm
  Includes bibliographical references.
  ISBN 978-1-62136-651-5 (trade paper) -- ISBN 978-1-62136-652-2
(e-book)
 1. Prayer--Christianity. 2. Bible--Prayers. I. Title.
  BV220.S665 2014
  242'.5--dc23

                    2014030834

First edition

14 15 16 17 18 — 9 8 7 6 5 4 3 2 1
Printed in the United States of America

CONTENTS

DEDICATION

*To my precious wife, Elizabeth. She and I have
prayed our way through many obstacles and have
seen the hand of God move...supernaturally.*

I would rather teach one man to
pray than ten men to preach.

[AUTHOR UNKNOWN]

INTRODUCTION

Around the turn of the millennium an intriguing megatrend swept across the body of Christ. Believers all around the globe became enthralled with an obscure, thirty-two-word prayer found in one verse of Scripture:

> And Jabez called on the God of Israel saying, "Oh, that You would bless me indeed, and enlarge my territory, that Your hand would be with me, and that You would keep me from evil, that I may not cause pain!"
> —1 Chronicles 4:10

I believe this brief petition resonated with millions of prayerful people primarily because of the concluding comment: *"So God granted him what he requested"* (1 Chron. 4:10, emphasis added).

Wow! How simple can you get? As far as we know Jabez didn't attend any all-night prayer vigils. No one laid hands on him so he could receive an impartation. He didn't fast forty days. He didn't prostrate himself before the Lord for hours. He didn't mechanically repeat a certain faith confession hundreds of times. These are not bad things to do, but they are not what Jabez did. He just made five short requests combined into one sentence that probably didn't take more than ten seconds to utter. And God was so deeply moved that He actually did it—*He granted him what he requested.* Don't you feel like echoing my sentiment? *Wow!*

I have to admit, I got swept away with the profound potency of this prayer too, but I can remember thinking to myself numerous times: "If Jabez's prayer could strike such awe in the hearts of believers, surely there are other prayers in the Bible that should also command our attention, prayers that are just as weighty (if not more so) and just as effective in securing a response from heaven."

So I embarked on a journey through God's Word, seeking not just instances in the Bible when people prayed, but specifically times when petitions also attracted some kind of supernatural response. I thought if certain prayer principles worked for celebrated faith heroes in the past, then using a similar approach should potentially bring results for believers who seek God in this era.

Well, I discovered a number of great examples—very inspiring prayers from key Bible figures such as Moses, Solomon, Jehoshaphat, Elijah, Jonah, and the members of the fledgling church in Jerusalem. Some are lengthy; some are quite short and to the point. But all were effective in bringing the kingdom of heaven down to earth.

Some of the prayers highlighted in this book have impacted me far more than the prayer of Jabez ever did— and studying them has awakened a renewed confidence that God will do it again. I pray the same thing happens for you.

Martin Luther is quoted as saying: "Prayer is not overcoming God's reluctance, but laying hold of His willingness."[1] Let me assure you, we are not trying to "force" God's hand by using these time-proven methods. Instead we are merely aligning ourselves with God's will and getting in a receptive position.

Recently I saw a sign outside an old country church that said it beautifully: "Prayer is the arms of the soul thrown around the neck of God." What spiritual abandon these words describe—approaching the Most High not with stiff, structured forms of prayer, but an all-consuming love that melts the heart!

Jesus commented to the Father: "Out of the mouth of babes and nursing infants You have perfected praise" (Matt. 21:16). Perfect praise is not practiced, polished, planned, or professional. It is passionate, original, spontaneous, sincere, enthusiastic, and full of life. May each chapter of this book be an incentive toward "perfect praise," not rigid rules of religious conduct.

In each chapter I highlight the "power points" of each prayer that we need to draw from and imitate. However, intentionally I have not written out the prayers for you (though there's nothing wrong with that). I want you to depend more on the Holy Spirit to grant you inspiration as you personalize each prayer to your unique set of circumstances.

Besides, prayer is not mechanical, it is relational. You don't come to God with formulas, you come to God with creative expressions of love and faith from your inner man. God is not a computer you program; He is your Father who loves you "with an everlasting love" (Jer. 31:3).

J. Hudson Taylor was used of God to bring a great revival in China in the 1800s, yet he admitted:

> Prayer power has never been tried to its full capacity.... If we want to see mighty wonders of divine power and grace

wrought in the place of weakness, failure and disappointment, let us answer God's standing challenge, "Call unto Me, and I will answer thee, and show thee great and mighty things which thou knowest not!"[2]

So let's accept this challenge together! Let's determine to achieve the "full capacity" of a consecrated prayer life, expecting "great and mighty things" (Jer. 33:3).

Prayer does not fit us for the greater work; prayer is the greater work.[1]

[OSWALD CHAMBERS]

Chapter 1

THE PRAYER OF MOSES

Please, show me Your glory.
Exodus 33:18

THE NAME MOSES means "drawn out." He was given this name because of the way he was rescued as a baby. Pharaoh had commanded the Hebrews to throw all newborn males into the river. Moses's mother, disregarding the dictate, placed her son in a basket that miraculously drifted right into the very area where Pharaoh's daughter bathed. (Surely angels were involved in that rescue!) When she saw the child, she had pity on him and *drew him out of the water.*

Miriam, Moses's sister, was standing close by, watching to see what would happen. She cleverly asked Pharaoh's daughter if she should go find a Hebrew woman who could nurse the child for her. Pharaoh's daughter agreed, so Miriam brought her own mother who ended up receiving wages to nurse *her own son* (how powerfully God orchestrated that!). So this baby destined for death was instead absorbed into the royal family and raised as Pharaoh's adopted son. Isn't God amazing?

Moses spent the first forty years of his life in Pharaoh's court. But then he was forced to flee Egypt after he was seen killing an Egyptian who had attacked a Hebrew slave.

He spent the next forty years in exile, tending sheep in the desert. Then God called Moses to return to Egypt to deliver the children of Israel out of slavery. Anyone who has seen *The Ten Commandments*, or other films depicting the exodus of the Israelites out of Egypt, can easily visualize the dramatic way God moved. After ten prophesied plagues, the Israelites were off to the wilderness, where God parted the Red Sea and protected them round-the-clock by a pillar of cloud by day and a pillar of fire by night.

You could say that during the first forty years of Moses's life in Pharaoh's court he learned to be *something*. During the second forty years spent in exile in the desert, Moses learned to be *nothing*. Then in the last forty years, after the burning bush encounter, Moses learned how God can take *nothing* and make *something* out of it. (See Hebrews 11:23–29.)

What Prompted Moses to Pray This Prayer?

When Exodus 32 begins, Moses was on Mount Sinai, receiving the Ten Commandments and additional revelations. The Israelites, taking advantage of his absence, lapsed into idolatry. They convinced Aaron to make them a golden calf to be their god and when Moses returned after forty days of fasting, they were dancing around the idol in a naked, demonized frenzy.

(As a side note, have you ever considered why the Israelites made a "calf" to worship? Why not another animal that is more impressive in its appearance? The answer reveals a flaw in their thinking; the cow is the main domestic animal that serves mankind, so the subtle message was that they wanted a "deity" who would serve them, not a God they were required to serve.)

Moses's first reaction was to throw down and break the tablets of stone, burn the idol, grind it to powder, mix it with water, and make the children of Israel drink of the concoction. After this Moses displayed great unselfishness. When God set His mind toward destroying the entire nation and raising up a new nation from Moses's seed, Moses pled with God to instead remember His commitment to Abraham, Isaac, and Jacob. God mercifully relented. Then heartbroken Moses prayed:

> Oh, these people have committed a great sin, and have made for themselves a god of gold! Yet now, if You will forgive their sin—but if not, I pray, blot me out of Your book which You have written.
>
> —EXODUS 32:31–32

God responded, "Whoever has sinned against Me, I will blot him out of My book" (v. 33). Then in Exodus 33 we find the Most High still deliberating over what He is going to do to the Israelites. At the same time, Moses, completely frustrated with the people, turns his heart worshipfully toward God:

> Then Moses said to the LORD, "See, You say to me, 'Bring up this people.' But You have not let me know whom You will send with me. Yet You have said, 'I know you by name, and you have also found grace in My sight.' Now therefore, I pray, if I have found grace in Your sight, show me now Your way, that I may know You and that I may find grace in Your sight. And consider that this nation is Your people."
>
> And He said, "My Presence will go with you, and I will give you rest."

Then he said to Him, "If Your Presence does not go with us, do not bring us up from here. For how then will it be known that Your people and I have found grace in Your sight, except You go with us? So we shall be separate, Your people and I, from all the people who are upon the face of the earth."

So the Lord said to Moses, "I will also do this thing that you have spoken; for you have found grace in My sight, and I know you by name."

And he said, "Please, show me Your glory."

—Exodus 33:12–18

God's Supernatural Response

This last petition that Moses uttered was only five words long (*"Please show me Your glory"*) but it elicited from God an extraordinary series of promises. Audibly He pledged:

"I will make all My goodness pass before you, and I will proclaim the name of the Lord before you. I will be gracious to whom I will be gracious, and I will have compassion on whom I will have compassion."

But He said, "You cannot see My face; for no man shall see Me, and live."

And the Lord said, "Here is a place by Me, and you shall stand on the rock.

So it shall be, while My glory passes by, that I will put you in the cleft of the rock, and will cover you with My hand while I pass by.

Then I will take away My hand, and you shall see My back; but My face shall not be seen."

—Exodus 33:19–23

God responded to Moses by giving him the very thing he asked. God showed him His glory. How amazing! And what He has done for one, He can do for another!

Four "Power Points" in Moses's Prayer

Now let's break down Moses's full conversation with God into four "power points" to see how and why he obtained such a visitation from the Most High.

Power point #1

> Now therefore, I pray, if I have found grace in Your sight, show me now Your way, that I may know You and that I may find grace in Your sight.
>
> —Exodus 33:13

Moses first asked to know God's "way," the God-inspired path that he should follow. He wanted to be in the center of God's will—because that's where the revelation of God's nature would come to him. He asked to know God's way, but his real passion was to know God's nature.

Knowing these two things would be a confirmation that grace had truly been applied to his life, but Moses requested this so that ultimately he could experience even *more* of the grace of God. The word translated "grace" is *chen* (pronounced khane), and it comes from a root word (*chanan*) that means to stoop down in order to help one who is inferior. Whenever God pours out grace, in a sense He "stoops down" from His level of holiness and perfection to help unholy and imperfect humanity, simply because He loves us.

Action step: *Ask God to pour out His grace in your life by leading you in the right path. But tell Him your highest passion is to know Him.*

Power point #2

> And consider that this nation is Your people.
>
> —Exodus 33:13

We are not just any people; we are the people of God. We belong to Him. We are "the Lord's portion" (Deut. 32:9), the group of people out of this world that He has inherited in a special relationship forever. So we, of all people, should expect His intervention.

Action step: *Declare to God that of all the people of the world, you are one of those who truly belong to Him.*

Power point #3

> If Your Presence does not go with us, do not bring us up from here. For how then will it be known that Your people and I have found grace in Your sight, except You go with us? So we shall be separate…from all the people who are upon the face of the earth.
>
> —Exodus 33:15–16

Moses made it clear that if they lost God's presence (the cloud by day, the fire by night, the supernatural fire on the altar that fell from heaven and the Shekinah glory cloud on the ark), they would lose the essence of who they were. It was the very thing that set them apart from all other nations. In essence he was saying, "If we lose that we might as well perish in the wilderness."

Action step: *Make it clear to God that His personal, abiding presence is infinitely more important to you than what He can do for you.*

Power point #4

Please, show me Your glory.

—EXODUS 33:18

The glory of God is His manifest presence—His great-ness, His dominion, His beauty, His awe-inspiring majesty and power. The term "glory" is translated from the Hebrew word *kabod*, which means heaviness or weight. To see the "glory" is to transcend this natural realm, to be lifted into a heavenly sphere, to behold the supernatural splendor of God. Sometimes this is experienced invisibly and internally, at other times it can be seen spilling over into the natural world. This "glory of God" is all the more available now for believers in the new covenant because of Jesus's death and resurrection:

> For it is the God who commanded light to shine out of darkness, who has shone in our hearts to give the light of the knowledge of *the glory of God* in the face of Jesus Christ.
> —2 CORINTHIANS 4:6, EMPHASIS ADDED

Action step: *Appeal to God to show you the glory of who He is and to manifest His glory in your life.*

My First Encounter With the Lord of Glory

I deeply relate to this passage of Scripture because it reminds me so much of how I first encountered the true and living God. You see, I haven't always been a believer in the unique-ness and exclusiveness of the Lord, Jesus Christ. In fact, at one time I taught that all religions were different paths to God.

In the early part of 1970 I was tired of the shallow-ness of my life and desperate to find ultimate reality. So I dropped out of Florida State University to study Kundalini yoga under an Indian guru. In the fall of that year I began teaching that same practice to about three hundred students at four universities in the Tampa, Florida, area. In a sense I was their "guru" (a word that simply means *teacher*). I was also running a yoga ashram, a commune where yoga devotees follow a more intense discipline. Each day I taught various techniques geared toward achieving that illusive state referred to in eastern religions as "God consciousness."

Every day began at 3:30 a.m. with two to three hours of meditation and mantra yoga (the chanting of mantras) then various yoga disciplines for about twelve hours. However, one unique and wonderful day I broke with my normal pattern. An old friend had written me a letter explaining that he had been "born again" (an unfamiliar concept to me at the time) and that he had discovered Jesus to be the only way to heaven. I initially responded in the negative, that I could not confine myself to Christianity. But my friend's letter weighed heavily on my mind.

So one morning I decided that instead of going through my usual yoga routine, I would spend the whole day praying *only* to Jesus and reading *only* the Bible. Though I was not aware of it at the time, I was using a "Moses-like" approach. All day I continually asked the Lord to reveal Himself, using words like the following:

> Lord Jesus, I dedicate this day to You. *Show me the way.* If there is such a thing as being "saved by *grace*," help me understand it. If You are truly *the only way* to eternal life, if You really died on the cross for my sins and rose again,

I pray You will reveal Yourself supernaturally. *Manifest Yourself.* Give me some kind of sign. I open my heart.

I didn't use any yoga methods that day. Instead I just called upon the name of the Lord, not knowing the promise in Romans 10:13, "Whoever calls on the name of the Lord shall be saved." When Moses prayed that God would reveal His gory, God's loving response was:

> I will make all My goodness pass before you, and I will proclaim the name of the LORD before you. I will be gracious to whom I will be gracious, and I will have compassion on whom I will have compassion.
>
> —EXODUS 33:19

A similar thing happened for me. After spending the whole day calling on Jesus, I had to leave to go teach a yoga class at the University of South Florida (USF). Because I'd made a commitment not to own any material things, I had to walk, hitchhike, or get a ride to my classes. That day when I stepped out on the road, I was still praying, *"Jesus, if You are the way, please show me today. Give me a supernatural sign."* I was fully expecting an answer.

About a mile away a new believer named Kent Sullivan was walking into a Laundromat to wash his dirty clothes. He was a student at USF and had converted to Christianity out of yoga and Eastern religions a few months before. Kent just "happened" to be a member of a prayer group that had been praying for me. Their leader had seen an article about me in the *Tampa Tribune* newspaper, so she cut it out, pinned it to their prayer board, and arranged for someone to be fasting and praying for me every hour of every day. Unknown to me, I was being "soaked" with intercession. Therefore what happened next was no "coincidence"; it was a prayer-propelled "God-incidence."

The Holy Spirit spoke to Kent's heart, "Get back in your van and start driving. I've got a job for you to do." Wondering why God had interrupted his plans, Kent went down the road, turning whenever he felt a "witness" in his spirit. After several turns he saw me standing on the side of the road with my thumb stuck out. He never picked up hitchhikers but felt strangely compelled to break his rule for me. He had no idea I was the yoga teacher his prayer group had been interceding for the previous month.

I opened the door and my heart began racing. On the ceiling Kent had taped a picture of Jesus. I knew it was my "sign." A few minutes later he said, "Can I ask you a question?" "Yes," I replied with excitement. "Have you ever asked Jesus into your heart?" he asked, radiating a big smile. Without hesitation I answered, "No, but when can I?" Kent was astonished at my eagerness.

Little did he realize the Holy Spirit had been preparing me for weeks for our encounter. Within a few minutes we were on our knees in the back of the van, and I was spiritually reborn. Once I accepted the Lord into my heart, I *knew* I was complete. I *knew* I finally had union with God, and I *knew* that I had finally found the truth. This internal *knowing* was immediate and undeniable. It was so transformational that I asked Kent to accompany me to my class at USF and to all my classes that week to help me explain what had happened to me and why my yoga courses were going to be discontinued from that point forward. (Incidentally, many of my students became Christians as well.)

That day in Kent's van something supernatural happened to me similar to Moses's supernatural encounter. God made His "*goodness*" pass before me (showing me the revelation of the crucifixion and resurrection of the Son of God).

The word *gospel* means "good news." As I learned various facets of the *good news*, the *goodness of the Lord kept passing before me again and again*—and I learned from the beginning, God's glory is His goodness.

When Moses asked to see God's glory, the second part of God's response was the pledge that He would "*proclaim the name of the Lord*" before Moses (Exod. 33:19, emphasis added). That happened to me also during that pivotal turning point. I learned the true name of the Lord was not Brahman (from Hinduism), or Sat Nam (from Sikhism) or Allah (from Islam)—but *the Lord Jesus Christ*, the triune name of the triune God, the name that is above every name, the name to which every knee will bow and every tongue will confess, the name that is connected to the true revelation of the plan of God for man.

Finally, at the close of Exodus 33 we find God doing something remarkable for Moses, something that speaks in a symbolic and spiritual way to us:

> And the LORD said, "Here is a place by Me, and you shall stand on the rock.
>
> So it shall be, while My glory passes by, that I will put you in the cleft of the rock, and will cover you with My hand while I pass by.
>
> Then I will take away My hand, and you shall see My back; but My face shall not be seen."
>
> —EXODUS 33:21–23

In like manner, when the Lord passed by me in the fall of 1970, He placed His hand upon me, opening up my spiritual understanding. In a spiritual sense He placed me in the "cleft of the Rock"—the One who is called the Rock of Ages. From that day forward I have been "hid with Christ in God" (Col. 3:3).

Several weeks later I was battling raging doubt in my mind over the concept that the Bible is actually God's inspired Word. The Lord Jesus understood my struggle and came to me in a dream. He appeared before me in glowing white apparel, so brilliant I could not make out the features of His face. Then He disappeared and in His place was the Bible, glowing with the same brilliant white light, with golden Hebrew print on the pages, and pulsating like it had a heartbeat. A river of light poured off the pages into my soul, and I realized that God and His Word are one and that the Bible truly is the Word of God. My doubts were dispelled forever when I beheld His glory!

Did all of these things happen because of prayer? Absolutely! Was it important that I asked God to show me His way (the right path) and manifest Himself to me supernaturally? Yes. It worked for Moses and it worked for me.

As Watchman Nee so aptly declared:

> Our prayers lay the track down on which God's power can come. Like a mighty locomotive, His power is irresistible, but it cannot reach us without rails.[2]

So lay down the rails today. You may be surprised what comes to you from above.

What About You?

Now it is time for you to pray, confess, and believe the "power points" in the Moses prayer. The following statements summarize what we have learned in this chapter. After rehearsing these points, create your own prayer using a similar approach. Use as many parts of the Moses prayer as you can, especially the four points specified. When you develop your prayer:

+ Remind God it was His grace alone that began a work in you.
+ Ask God to lead you into His way, the path of truth.
+ Tell God your greatest passion is to know Him, not just know about Him.
+ Request more grace in His sight.
+ Declare to God that of all the people of the world, you are one of those who truly belong to Him.
+ Make it clear to God that His personal, abiding presence is infinitely more important to you than what He can do for you.
+ Ask God to show you His glory!

Lord God of Moses, [complete your prayer as the Holy Spirit leads, drawing as needed from the statements above].

Chapter 2

THE PRAYER OF HANNAH

O LORD of hosts, if You will indeed look on the
affliction of Your maidservant and remember me...

1 SAMUEL 1:11

AROUND 1100 BC there was a man who lived in the mountains of Ephraim named Elkanah. He had two wives, Peninah, whose name means *pearl*, and Hannah, whose name means *grace, gracious,* or *favored.* Ironically Hannah was the one who did *not* seem favored, for she was barren, which was considered a sign of a curse, especially in that era. Peninah, who was blessed with offspring, taunted Hannah unmercifully, knowing how desperately she wanted a child. This went on for years.

Each year Elkanah went to Shiloh to worship at the tabernacle, and during one of those pilgrimages Hannah reached an impasse. No longer able to endure the pain of her own heart and the ridicule of her rival, Peninah, Hannah went to the tent of meeting to seek God for an answer. Here's the biblical account:

> So Hannah arose after they had finished eating and drinking in Shiloh. Now Eli the priest was sitting on the seat by the doorpost of the tabernacle of the LORD.

And she was in bitterness of soul, and prayed to the LORD and wept in anguish.

Then she made a vow and said, *"O Lord of hosts, if You will indeed look on the affliction of Your maidservant and remember me, and not forget Your maidservant, but will give Your maidservant a male child, then I will give him to the Lord all the days of his life, and no razor shall come upon his head."*

And it happened, as she continued praying before the LORD, that Eli watched her mouth.

Now Hannah spoke in her heart; only her lips moved, but her voice was not heard. Therefore Eli thought she was drunk.

So Eli said to her, "How long will you be drunk? Put your wine away from you!"

But Hannah answered and said, "No, my lord, I am a woman of sorrowful spirit. I have drunk neither wine nor intoxicating drink, but have poured out my soul before the LORD.

"Do not consider your maidservant a wicked woman, for out of the abundance of my complaint and grief I have spoken until now."

Then Eli answered and said, "Go in peace, and the God of Israel grant your petition which you have asked of Him."

And she said, "Let your maidservant find favor in your sight." So the woman went her way and ate, and her face was no longer sad.

Then they rose early in the morning and worshiped before the LORD, and returned and came to their house at Ramah. And Elkanah knew Hannah his wife, and the LORD remembered her.

So it came to pass in the process of time that Hannah

conceived and bore a son, and called his name Samuel, saying, "Because I have asked for him from the Lord."

—1 Samuel 1:9–20, emphasis added

Hannah was driven to such a point of desperation that she made a very serious vow to God: if God gave her a son, she would give that child back to Him to serve at the tabernacle. The Lord of hosts heard her cry, opened her womb, and blessed her with a son. She called him Samuel, which means *His name is El*, or possibly, *asked of God*, or *heard of God* because he came forth in response to prayer. A man passionate for the truth, Samuel became one of the most revered prophets, judges, and faith heroes in the Bible.

Prayerful Hannah had a far greater impact on Israel in her day than anyone could have possibly recognized at the time. After God gave Hannah her long-awaited son, she authored a ten-verse hymn of thanksgiving to God, which is considered one of the most magnificent prophetic poems in the Bible (1 Sam. 2:1–10). Certain parts are quite similar to the ten-verse outburst of praise that flowed from the Virgin Mary many centuries later (Luke 1:46–55). In this song Hannah also became the first person in Scripture to call the coming promised seed the "Messiah" (translated in 1 Samuel 2:10 as "His anointed," from the Hebrew *maschiach*, meaning "Messiah"). Hannah's prayer, God's answer, and her song of praise all witness powerfully to God's supernatural provision, both for Hannah and mankind.

God's Supernatural Response

The primary, immediate supernatural "event" was Hannah becoming pregnant with her son Samuel. She who was "barren" became a "joyful mother of children"—by divine intervention (Ps. 113:9). However, there were numerous aftereffects resulting from her faith that covered much more territory.

At that time, the priesthood had become very corrupt. Eli, the high priest, was old, obese, and somewhat insensitive to the importance of his position. Avoiding confrontation, he refused to restrain his sons, Hophni and Phinehas—who were described in Scripture as "sons of Belial" (1 Sam. 2:12, KJV; according to Smith's Bible Dictionary, Belial is a name for Satan meaning worthlessness or lawlessness, thus "sons of Belial" are "sons of the devil, sons of the worthless and lawless one"—thus, they tend to live worthless and lawless lives themselves). Hophni and Phinehas continuously defiled the priesthood through their sensuality, drunkenness, and blasphemous disrespect toward sacred things. Regrettably, God's people could go no further than their backslidden leaders, so Israel was careening downhill into an abyss of spiritual darkness. God had to intervene, but He needed an intercessor.

Hannah kept her commitment and after Samuel was "weaned" she brought him to Eli to be reared under his tutelage. It is a miracle of divine preservation that Samuel was able to grow up around such corruption and still remain pure. When he was old enough to comprehend the calling, God visited him with a prophetic word foretelling the severe judgments that would soon fall on the house of Eli. It happened, and Eli and his rebellious sons, Hophni and Phinehas, died in one day.

The spiritual authority in Israel then shifted to Samuel. Because of his righteous walk with God as a prophet and a judge, he led the Israelites into an era of national revival, a time of greater revelation of truth and fervency toward the

God of Abraham. He was also the one used of God to usher in the reign of kings, anointing Saul and later David, who brought forth the dynasty that would produce the Messiah, the King of all kings, who will one day manifestly rule the entire world. So profoundly important things ultimately leading to global transformation resulted from one woman who "poured out her soul before the Lord" (1 Sam. 1:15).

Also to be noted is the last verse of Hannah's celebrated prophetic psalm:

> The adversaries of the Lord shall be broken in pieces; from heaven He will thunder against them.
>
> — 1 Samuel 2:10

This was fulfilled many years later in the life and ministry of Samuel, during a battle with the Philistines:

> Now as Samuel was offering up the burnt offering, the Philistines drew near to battle against Israel. But the Lord *thundered with a loud thunder* upon the Philistines that day, and so confused them that they were overcome before Israel.
>
> —1 Samuel 7:10, emphasis added

So the prophetic word she received was not fulfilled in her life but in the life of her son. Sometimes it happens like that.

Four "Power-Points" in Hannah's Prayer

In the prayer of Hannah are four important power points. Let's ponder each.

Power point #1

> O Lord of hosts…
>
> —1 Samuel 1:11

The story of Hannah is the first place in Scripture where this name for God is found. To honor Him as the "Lord of hosts" is to declare that He is the God of multitudes of angels that constantly do His bidding. Angels are not only agents of worship toward God, they are also spirit beings who "do His pleasure" and who "make war" against satanic forces in order to displace them. (See Psalm 103:21; Revelation 12:7–8.) They are also described as God's "ministers" who "excel in strength" and "[heed] the voice of His word" (Ps. 103:20–21). All through the Bible we read of angelic intervention in the lives of God's people.

Action step: *Honor God worshipfully as the Lord of hosts and expect angelic intervention in your circumstances.*

Power point #2

> If You will indeed look on the affliction of Your maidservant...
>
> —1 SAMUEL 1:11

With this line Hannah went beyond the earthly high priest and invited God to be personally involved in her pain. He does that. Hebrews 4:15 even promises that we have a High Priest who is "touched with the feeling of our infirmities" (KJV); the New King James Version declares that He sympathizes "with our weaknesses." One of the most powerful verses in the Bible to claim in this area is Psalm 34:19, "Many are the afflictions of the righteous, but the LORD delivers him out of them all."

Action step: *Ask God to look on the areas of affliction in your life and pray that He will be touched with the "feeling" of your infirmities.*

Power point #3

Remember me, and not forget Your maidservant...
—I SAMUEL 1:11

God is never challenged with His memory (even though He is "the Ancient of Days"). He has full recall. "There is no searching of His understanding" (Isa. 40:28, KJV). And powerful, supernatural things happen when God brings His people to remembrance, such as:

- **Noah's deliverance from the ark:** "Then *God remembered Noah*, and every living thing, and all the animals that were with him in the ark. And God made a wind to pass over the earth, and the waters subsided" (Gen. 8:1, emphasis added).

- **Lot's deliverance from Sodom:** "*God remembered Abraham*, and sent Lot out of the midst of the overthrow...." (Gen. 19:29, emphasis added). Because Lot was Abraham's nephew, and God was in covenant with Abraham, there was an overflow of mercy toward Lot and his family that caused them to be rescued when God destroyed Sodom and Gomorrah.

- **Israel's deliverance from Egypt:** "Now it happened in the process of time that the king of Egypt died. Then the children of Israel groaned because of the bondage, and they cried out; and their cry came up to God because of the bondage. So God heard their groaning, *and God remembered His covenant with Abraham, with Isaac, and with Jacob*" (Exod. 2:23–24, emphasis added). From that point forward great supernatural intervention took place to get God's people to the Promised Land.

This reassuring truth is revealed in Hebrews 6:10, "For God is not unjust [the King James Version says "unrighteous"] to forget your work and labor of love which you have shown toward His name." So if God failed to remember His covenant with you and your faithfulness toward Him, He would consider it an unjust and unrighteous thing. "Remembering" is a part of His ethical and moral character base. How comforting it is to know that this is not just a temporary expectation for us, for "the righteous will be in everlasting remembrance" (Ps. 112:6).

Action step: *Ask God to remember your dilemma, to remember His covenant with you, to remember you eternally, and not to forget your "work and labor of love" toward His name.*

Power point #4

> But will give Your maidservant a male child, then I will give him to the Lord all the days of his life, and no razor shall come upon his head.
> —1 Samuel 1:11

Hannah promised God that if He would bless her with a son, that same son would be dedicated to His service and be a Nazarite from the womb. She promised if God would give to her that she would give back to Him. He rewarded her with more children after that as a result, for the Scripture says, "Give, and it will be given to you" (Luke 6:38).

Action step: *Tell God that whatever He blesses you with, you will return it to Him and dedicate to Him to bless His kingdom.*

A Miracle Like Hannah's

Because of a condition in her body, my wife, Elizabeth, and I were told that we would never have children. But God had the last word. Months before when He had told me that it was time for us to marry, He also informed me that we would have a son. So I believed the "report of the Lord" and not the report of man (Isa. 53:1). I praised the Lord for our son in advance and called those things that were not as though they were. It wasn't too long before my wife was pregnant.

The battle was not over, though; big challenges were still ahead. When Elizabeth was giving birth to our son, she was in labor for about forty-eight hours. When it finally came time for him to be born, Elizabeth was completely drained of all strength. Consequently, Zion Seth laid in the birth canal for a dangerously long time and finally had to be pulled out with forceps.

Later that day certain hospital counselors visited us to let us know they would be sending a support team to our home for numerous visits during the next few months. They explained that our son had suffered severe oxygen deprivation during the birthing process and that they were sure he had suffered serious and irreparable brain damage. They forecast that he would be severely developmentally delayed and possibly physically handicapped and that we needed to prepare ourselves to cope with that. How did we react? We respectfully declined their offer to counsel us and set ourselves to seek the Lord, rededicating Zion Seth to God (as we had done many times before his birth) and praying that God would supernaturally intervene.

Part of the miracle must have happened right away while

another part did not transpire for years. As he grew, our son never showed any signs of brain damage. In fact, eighteen years later when he went to college, he was placed in the highest honors society available to freshmen at Lee University.

However, when he was about eight years old there was a lingering physical problem that God finally resolved. Up until that time Seth had always been a toe-walker. He never walked flat-footed. We tried everything. Finally in desperation we went to an orthopedic hospital in Atlanta, where a very kind doctor informed us the only thing he could do was cut the tendons in his heels and hope for the best. There was a fifty-fifty chance that the tendons would grow back longer. If it didn't work, Seth would be damaged for life.

I felt God told me not to resort to that approach, so we left. Instead, at a conference a few months later two other ministers joined with me in praying over my son for about twenty minutes, decreeing that he be healed. When we set him down on his feet, he began walking flatfooted and has never walked on his toes habitually since.

Our daughter was an even greater faith-challenge. About five months into the pregnancy, our OB/GYN said our daughter had spina bifida (a hole in the spine) and cretinism (severe developmental delay). After showing us the ultrasound that would prove his findings, he leaned over his desk and said, "There is an alternative." We knew what he was implying: abortion, which as far as we were concerned was a totally unacceptable choice. So we walked out never intending to return.

Brokenhearted, my wife was praying her heart as we left, totally overwhelmed. She started reminding God that we had dedicated this child to Him. Suddenly she heard her Father's audible voice say: "Your daughter will dance on the streets of Jerusalem!"

The doctor had just informed us she probably wouldn't walk, but God said she would dance. Intense spiritual warfare was going on. When we got in our vehicle, we received a double confirmation. Elizabeth turned on the radio, and the first song to come on was "I Hope You Dance." She started praising God then and there.

For the remaining months of the pregnancy we constantly "declared the decree," echoing what God had spoken to us (Ps. 2:7). We prophetically named our daughter Destiny Hope as a way of counteracting the prognosis that she had no hope. Many times a day Elizabeth would sing "I Hope You Dance" to the child in her womb. She would also quote Psalm 138:8 often, laying her hands on her belly, confessing: "The LORD will perfect that which concerns me."

And it worked. Our little princess was born perfect. And, by the way, she dances.

We dedicated both our children to God, and against all odds both came forth miraculously—and God is still working miracles in their lives.

God remembered us. He remembered our commitment to Him. He remembered our covenant with Him. He remembered the promises of His Word. He did not forget the work of His hands.

What About You?

Now it is time for you to pray, confess, and believe the four power points in the Hannah prayer. The following bulleted statements summarize what we have learned in this chapter. After rehearsing these points, create your own prayer using a similar approach. Use as many parts of the Hannah prayer as you can, especially the four points specified:

+ Declare that your God is the Lord of hosts (the God of a multitude of angels).
+ Pray that He will commission His "ministering spirits" to intervene supernaturally on your behalf.
+ Ask God to gaze into your life, to look upon you, especially any areas of affliction you are facing.
+ Pray that He will be touched with the "feeling" of your infirmities.
+ Ask God to remember you, your commitment to Him, and His covenant with you.
+ Make a commitment to God that everything He blesses you with, you will return to Him (just as Hannah returned Samuel). Inform your heavenly Father that everything you presently have, or ever will have, is and ever will be for His glory and for the advance of His kingdom.

Now it's your turn to pray:

Lord God of Hannah, [complete your prayer as the Holy Spirit leads, drawing as needed from the bullet points above].

Chapter 3

THE PRAYER OF SOLOMON #1

*Now give me wisdom and knowledge, that I may
go out and come in before this people; for who
can judge this great people of Yours?*

2 CHRONICLES 1:10

SOLOMON'S HISTORY IS told in 1 Kings 1–11 and 2 Chronicles 1–9. He was David's eighth son and the heir of his throne (another example of God causing the last to be first). Solomon had an artistic side. He loved literature and magnificent architecture. First Kings 4:32 claims that he wrote 3,000 proverbs and composed 1,005 songs, but many of these proverbs are no longer available to us, and most of the songs have been buried in the past. Only two psalms have been attributed to him: Psalm 72 and Psalm 127.

In his writings Solomon covered a wide spectrum, authoring Ecclesiastes (one of the gloomiest books in the Bible) and the Song of Solomon (by far, the most glorious glimpse of the beauty of the bride of Christ). Though noted for his gift of wisdom, in his latter years he lived very foolishly. As a result, great instability overtook the kingdom of Israel.

Growing up in the shadow of King David must have been challenging for Solomon. As a child, he must have wondered how he could ever hope to measure up to such an icon of courage and conquest. But the pressure would only increase. When David passed to the land of his fathers, the full weight of the kingdom came down on Solomon's shoulders. All eyes were on him. Every decision he made affected the entire nation. Overwhelmed by his new charge, Solomon was driven to seek God, asking Him for wisdom and knowledge.

> Now the bronze altar that Bezalel the son of Uri, the son of Hur, had made, he put before the tabernacle of the LORD; Solomon and the assembly sought Him there. And Solomon went up there to the bronze altar before the LORD, which was at the tabernacle of meeting, and offered a thousand burnt offerings on it.
>
> On that night God appeared to Solomon, and said to him, "Ask! What shall I give you?"
>
> And Solomon said to God: *"You have shown great mercy to David my father, and have made me king in his place. Now, O LORD God, let Your promise to David my father be established, for You have made me king over a people like the dust of the earth in multitude. Now give me wisdom and knowledge, that I may go out and come in before this people; for who can judge this great people of Yours?"*
>
> Then God said to Solomon: "Because this was in your heart, and you have not asked riches or wealth or honor or the life of your enemies, nor have you asked long life—but have asked wisdom and knowledge for yourself, that you may judge My people over whom I have made you king—wisdom and knowledge are granted to you; and I will give you riches and wealth and honor, such as none of the kings have had who were before you, nor shall any after you have the like."
>
> So Solomon came to Jerusalem from the high place

that was at Gibeon, from before the tabernacle of meeting, and reigned over Israel.

—2 Chronicles 1:5–13, emphasis added

Quite extravagant in His approach to the Lord, Solomon offered a thousand burnt offerings on the brazen altar. That type of sacrifice (animals reduced to ashes on an altar) was a symbol that the person giving the offering was wholly consumed with devotion to God. We are about to see that Solomon attracted God's attention with his sincere and excessive worship—and he reaped tremendous benefits.

God's Supernatural Response

God gave an immediate response to Solomon's prayer, prophesying that he would receive more than what he asked for—granting him "riches, and wealth and honor" (2 Chron. 1:12). Shortly after receiving his gift, Solomon demonstrated great wisdom in how he dealt with two women who were fighting over who was the rightful mother of a living child (1 Kings 3:16–28). When he resolved the delicate issue with spiritual finesse, "all Israel heard of the judgment which the king had rendered; and they feared the king, for they saw that the wisdom of God was in him to administer justice" (1 Kings 3:28). So supernaturally, by a God-given gift, he was given sway over a multitude of people that might have been quite difficult to manage otherwise.

But that was just the beginning. Solomon's influence was felt internationally. His fame spread throughout the world. Eventually he became so renowned for his gift of wisdom that notable persons such as the Queen of Sheba traveled from afar to hear his words (2 Chron. 9:1–12).

Three "Power Points" in Solomon's Prayer

Let's look at three power points revealed in Solomon's prayer.

Power point #1

> You have shown great mercy to David my father, and have
> made me king in his place.
> —2 Chronicles 1:8

Solomon first celebrated the magnanimous mercy of God evidenced in his father's life. One of the greatest signs that God's mercy poured over David was the very fact that Solomon, his son, was chosen to occupy his throne. Of all David's sons Solomon was the least likely candidate, being the product of what was originally an illicit, adulterous union concealed by a murderous plot.

No question about it—Solomon should have inherited a curse from David and Bathsheba; instead, he inherited a kingdom. The Scripture centuries before had prophesied that God visits "the iniquity of the fathers upon the children to the third and fourth generations" (Deut. 5:9). Had this been enforced, Solomon would have been an outcast from the presence of the Almighty. Instead, he was gifted as an oracle of God—striding into the ranks of about forty authors who were used by the Holy Spirit over a period of fifteen hundred years to produce that glorious compilation of God-breathed writings we call the Holy Bible.

Though he could have never fully comprehended the ultimate results of this outpoured favor, it is obvious that Solomon was filled with gratitude for what he did know. It's as if the hand of God wrote over his life, "mercy triumphs over judgment" (James 2:13)—for he was even included in the royal lineage that would one day bring forth the Messiah (Jesus, the Son of God *spiritually*, was also the son of David and of Solomon *naturally*).

Instead of boasting of his newly assigned position of authority, Solomon humbly attributed all the glory to God. He insisted that it was all the mercy of God. We should cultivate the same attitude.

Action step: *Declare to God that everything you are is the result of His mercy, that you should have been a slave to sin eternally. Rejoice that instead, like Solomon, you are reigning as a king with the Lord.*

Power point #2

> Now, O Lord God, let Your promise to David my father be established, for You have made me king over a people like the dust of the earth in multitude.
>
> —2 Chronicles 1:9

Solomon cast all his hopes for the future on a promise God made in the past. In Psalm 132:11 the divine pledge was affirmed, "The Lord has sworn in truth to David; He will not turn from it: 'I will set upon your throne the fruit of your body.'"

Solomon was also acknowledging how heavy the responsibility of his position really was—for the Israelites are like "the dust of the earth." By highlighting the largeness of the task, and implying his inability to accomplish it, this freshly inaugurated king is appealing to the Lord of the universe to partner with him. He didn't place himself in such a position of honor and influence; God's promise did! Therefore, the One who authored such a calling in him would surely sustain him and empower him to carry out his charge.

Action step: *Acknowledge three things: first, that your life is a product of the promises of God; second, that you didn't really choose God, He chose you; and third, that the responsibility you have inherited as a child of God is larger than you can handle. Then appeal to God to partner with you in all you attempt for His glory.*

Power point #3

> Now give me wisdom and knowledge, that I may go out and come in before this people; for who can judge this great people of Yours?
> —2 Chronicles 1:10

Biblically, knowledge is information, understanding, or revelation collected over a period of time through a real relationship with God. It results from the study of His Word and the experience of life itself. Wisdom is the ability to apply that knowledge in such a way that both we and the world around us are benefitted. If a person lacks knowledge, he or she will lack wisdom also: the two always walk hand in hand.

Solomon testified that "the fear of the Lord" is both "the beginning of knowledge" and "the beginning of wisdom" (Prov. 1:7; 9:10). So no one can experience true, lasting knowledge or wisdom without taking this initial step of embracing a high degree of trembling devotion and reverential awe toward God.

Wisdom is a gift offered freely to all believers, as the following scripture attests:

> If any of you lacks wisdom, let him ask of God, who gives to all liberally and without reproach, and it will be given to him. But let him ask in faith, with no doubting, for he

who doubts is like a wave of the sea driven and tossed by the wind.

—James 1:5–6

The Holy Spirit is referred to as both the "spirit of knowledge" and the "spirit of wisdom" (Isa. 11:2; Eph. 1:17), so when we are filled with the Holy Spirit and when we "walk in the Spirit" (Gal. 5:16, 25), these two divine attributes should automatically be expressed in us and through us. Our God is "a God of knowledge" and "the only wise God" (1 Sam. 2:3; 1 Tim. 1:17). Fellowship with Him causes a reflection of His nature to emerge in us.

Two of the nine supernatural gifts of the Holy Spirit are "the word of knowledge" and "the word of wisdom" (1 Cor. 12:8). These are flashes of divine insight that give a believer a supernatural advantage in ministering to others in business, in relationships, in religion and spirituality, in life as a whole—for we comprehend things from God's perspective.

Solomon addressed God with the statement, "Who can judge such a great people as Yours?" (2 Chron. 1:10). In doing this, he acknowledged that the people belong to God, not to him. In like manner, we need to acknowledge that our businesses, careers, families, money, possessions, ministries, even our callings—all these actually belong to God. We are only stewards watching over that which He owns. We should echo the words Jesus used as He ended the Lord's Prayer, "Yours is the kingdom, the power and the glory" (Matt. 6:13).

Action step: *Ask for wisdom and knowledge, not for your own sake but for the sake of others. Then tell God that everything you have naturally and spiritually actually belongs to Him.*

Impacting an Entire Nation

It was the fall of 1997. I was taking an ordinary plane trip. Unknown to me, God had injected into my fairly predictable routine something quite extraordinary that would change the course of a nation and impact the lives of thousands of people.

About thirty minutes into the flight an African man, short in stature and wearing regal traditional dress, walked out of the first class section into the coach area where I was sitting. I noticed he was moving slowly and gazing intently at each passenger as he worked his way down the aisle. I had no idea God had given him a "word of wisdom," revealing that he was to go into the coach section because there was someone there he needed to talk with. After locking eyes with me, he stalled for a moment. Then sensing that inward "witness" he asked if he could sit down.

At that time, George Kiadii was an ambassador-at-large to the United States from the nation of Liberia. For a long time he had been praying that God would give him the necessary wisdom and knowledge to help rebuild his broken nation. It was a pivotal time in their troubling history. After seven years of civil war peace had finally been restored and free elections were scheduled to occur. To say that years of conflict had decimated that nation would be an understatement. Five rebel factions had fought one another for control of the country. So many lives were destroyed; so much beauty was irreparably marred.

This friendly stranger started off by introducing himself and explaining a little about who he was and why he was in the country. I informed him I was a Pentecostal minister and that I had done missionary work in Africa in the past.

He was delighted and excitedly responded that he was also a born-again, Spirit-filled minister of the gospel as well as a government representative. We discussed the Bible and shared personal stories. The camaraderie was remarkable. After a couple of hours our plane arrived at its destination, and we parted ways.

I never thought I would hear from Ambassador Kiadii again. Then about two months later he called my office and exclaimed, "My brother, we have finally had free elections. We have an elected president, senate, and congress now. Everything is changing. God has spoken that you must come and hold a Healing of the Nation Crusade in our capital city of Monrovia." I responded, "Brother, for an event that monumental you need someone better known in Africa." He would not be dissuaded, insisting that God had given him a "word of knowledge" (1 Cor. 12:8) about the meeting and that I was to be the primary speaker.

He explained that the meeting would be based on 2 Chronicles 7:14. The passage is actually very connected to this story of Solomon, being part of a revelation God spoke to him later on, after the dedication of the temple. It declares:

> If My people who are called by My name will humble themselves, and pray and seek My face, and turn from their wicked ways, then I will hear from heaven, and will forgive their sin and *heal their land.*
>
> —2 Chronicles 7:14, emphasis added

I prayed about it, and God said to go. An exorbitant amount of preparation had to be done because of the devastation caused by the war. We even purchased and shipped a sound system from New York to accommodate the crowd in Antoinette Tubman Stadium.

From the moment we arrived it was like a whirlwind of favor-driven activity. A large welcoming committee met us at the airport, including dozens of reporters intent on highlighting this pivotal national gathering.

The first night we had about twenty-five hundred people in the stadium (many people were still reluctant to come out of their houses at night because of the violence that had wracked the land for years). Still, notable things happened. Well over a thousand people prayed to be saved and filled with the Holy Spirit. The mayor of Monrovia sat on the platform, along with Madam Victoria, the only surviving president from the previous seven years, who came with her entourage of assistants. All of them humbly and sincerely prayed for salvation when the altar call was given. As we returned to the motel that night, we had to weave our way through hundreds of people dancing in the streets, joyously singing the gospel songs they had heard at the stadium.

The next day I received a phone call at my motel from the head of the senate. He asked me to come and address the recently installed congress. He wanted me to discuss how to implement biblical principles in governing the people so they might be able to wisely steer their faltering nation back to a place of stability. By the end of the week the open-air meeting grew to about thirty-five thousand people, and one of the major Muslim leaders in the country was saved.

However, one of the most amazing things happened *after* the meeting was over. The elected president, Charles Taylor (a controversial figure to say the least), made a national proclamation encouraging all citizens of Liberia to join him on a seven-day fast asking God to forgive their sin and heal their land. He invited the twenty-four supporting pastors who had helped organize our crusade to come and live with him in the presidential mansion for a week and do nothing day and night but seek the face of God. I was informed that he even placed guards at the door to prevent any government agents or business people from passing through those doors during that time.

After the crusade and that weeklong vigil, revival broke out and spread like wildfire across the nation. Ambassador Kiaddii told me shortly afterward that within about a month, roughly 183 new churches were formed, registering with the government and joining a national fellowship of evangelical churches. And it all happened because one man prayed for wisdom and knowledge and dared to act on "words of wisdom and knowledge" when God gave them to him.

What About You?

Now it is time for you to pray, confess, and believe the power points in Solomon's wisdom prayer. The following bulleted statements summarize what we have learned in this chapter. After rehearsing these points, create your own prayer drawing from these concepts. Use as many parts of the Solomon prayer as you can, especially the three points specified.

+ Declare to God that everything you have accomplished in life and everything you are is the result of His mercy.

+ Worshipfully celebrate specific times mercy prevailed in your life.

+ Admit that you should have been a slave to sin, but now you are reigning as a king, seated with Christ in heavenly places.

+ Proclaim that your life as a Christian is a product of the promises of God.

+ Declare that it was the almighty God who chose you.

+ Envision the greatness of your responsibility and ask God to partner with you in this endeavor, leading you and empowering you.

+ Ask God for wisdom and knowledge: a supernatural awakening of the mind of Christ within you, for in Him "are hidden all the treasures of wisdom and knowledge" (Col. 2:3).

+ Emphasize that you are asking, not just for your own sake but for the benefit of God's kingdom and for others.

Remember, even as God appeared to Solomon personally saying, "Ask. What shall I give you?" so God has come to all of us through His Son Jesus and is saying once again, "Ask, and it will be given to you" (Matt. 7:7).

Now it's your turn to pray:

Lord God of Solomon, [compose your prayer as the Holy Spirit leads, drawing as needed from the bullet points above].

Chapter 4

THE PRAYER OF SOLOMON #2

LORD God of Israel, there is no God in heaven or on earth like You, who keep Your covenant and mercy with Your servants who walk before You with all their hearts.

2 CHRONICLES 6:14

A s NOTED IN the previous chapter, Solomon was the last son of David. At the time he prayed the words recorded in 2 Chronicles 6, many years of war were over for the nation of Israel, and the dire consequences for David's time of backsliding had subsided. Apparently David the warrior king just wanted peace, so he named his final heir Solomon, meaning "peace." His name also identifies him with the capital city Jerusalem, which means "possession of peace" or "foundation of peace."[1]

Born around 1035 BC, Solomon was the second son of Bathsheba (her first son, the result of David's adultery, died shortly after birth). Solomon was raised under the prophet Nathan's oversight, who called him Jedidiah (meaning "beloved of the Lord"). Because of this relationship, Solomon probably had more spiritual influence in his life than any of David's other children. He reigned over Israel for forty years.

David longed to personally build a temple for the ark of the Lord, but God prevented him from doing so because he had "shed much blood on the earth" (1 Chron. 22:8). So he pursued the next best thing, doing everything possible to make preparations so his son could do it. He laid up all the needed materials (gold, silver, brass, precious stones). Then he commissioned Solomon to build the temple. Construction continued from the fourth through the eleventh years of Solomon's reign.

Here is the account of the magnificent manifestation that took place at the dedication:

> Then Solomon stood before the altar of the LORD in the presence of all the assembly of Israel, and spread out his hands (for Solomon had made a bronze platform five cubits long, five cubits wide, and three cubits high, and had set it in the midst of the court; and he stood on it, knelt down on his knees before all the assembly of Israel, and spread out his hands toward heaven); and he said: *"LORD God of Israel, there is no God in heaven or on earth like You, who keep Your covenant and mercy with Your servants who walk before You with all their hearts. You have kept what You promised Your servant David my father; You have both spoken with Your mouth and fulfilled it with Your hand, as it is this day. Therefore, LORD God of Israel, now keep what You promised Your servant David my father, saying, 'You shall not fail to have a man sit before Me on the throne of Israel, only if your sons take heed to their way, that they walk in My law as you have walked before Me.' And now, O LORD God of Israel, let Your word come true, which You have spoken to Your servant David.*
>
> *"But will God indeed dwell with men on the earth? Behold, heaven and the heaven of heavens cannot contain You. How much less this temple which I have built! Yet regard the prayer of Your servant and his supplication, O LORD my God, and listen to the cry and the prayer which Your servant is praying before You: that Your eyes may be open toward*

this temple day and night, toward the place where You said You would put Your name, that You may hear the prayer which Your servant makes toward this place.

"And may You hear the supplications of Your servant and of Your people Israel, when they pray toward this place … and when You hear, forgive …

Now, my God, I pray, let Your eyes be open and let Your ears be attentive to the prayer made in this place.

"Now therefore, arise, O Lord God, to Your resting place, You and the ark of Your strength. Let Your priests, O Lord God, be clothed with salvation, and let Your saints rejoice in goodness.

"O Lord God, do not turn away the face of Your Anointed; remember the mercies of Your servant David."

—2 Chronicles 6:12–21, 40–42, emphasis added

Awe-inspiring, supernatural manifestations were about to happen—yet God waited until the prayer was prayed. As John Wesley so aptly stated: "God does nothing except in response to believing prayer."[2]

God's Supernatural Response

Just prior to the time Solomon uttered this petition, the glory of God had already moved in such depth that the priests collapsed under the supernatural presence of God's Spirit. Here is the account:

And it came to pass when the priests came out of the Most Holy Place … and the Levites who were the singers, all those of Asaph and Heman and Jeduthun, with their sons and their brethren, stood at the east end of the altar, clothed in white linen, having cymbals, stringed instruments and harps, and with them one hundred and twenty priests sounding with trumpets—indeed it came to pass, when the trumpeters and singers were as one, to make one sound to be heard in praising and thanking the LORD, and when they lifted up their voice with the trumpets and cymbals and instruments of music, and praised the LORD, saying: "For He is good, for His mercy endures forever," that the house, the house of the LORD, was filled with a cloud, so that the priests could not continue ministering ["could not stand to minister" in the KJV] because of the cloud; for the glory of the LORD filled the house of God.

—2 CHRONICLES 5:11–14

That visitation at the beginning of the dedication service was powerful enough to be recorded in the annals of the history of God's dealings with mankind. But the intensity of what God's people experienced *after* Solomon's prayer was even more astounding:

When Solomon had finished praying, fire came down from heaven and consumed the burnt offering and the sacrifices; and the glory of the LORD filled the temple. And the priests could not enter the house of the LORD, because the glory of the LORD had filled the LORD's house. When all the children of Israel saw how the fire came down, and the glory of the LORD on the temple, they bowed their faces to the ground on the pavement, and worshiped and praised the LORD, saying: "For He is good, for His mercy endures forever."

—2 CHRONICLES 7:1–3

Initially they could not stand because of the glory of God's presence; by the end of the dedication they could not even enter the temple area because of the intensity of God's presence. And if that happened when the symbolic old covenant foreshadowing took place, how much more glorious it should be for the *fulfillment*: the living, new covenant temple of God worldwide.

When God answered Solomon's prayer, He made the following promise:

> Now My eyes will be open and My ears attentive to prayer made in this place. For now I have chosen and sanctified this house, that My name may be there forever; and My eyes and My heart will be there perpetually.
>
> —2 Chronicles 7:15–16

The temple of Solomon was just a symbol of God's true and ultimate intention—to make believers His living temple. If He would give this pledge concerning an inanimate building, how much more will He speak over the "living stones" that make up His worldwide spiritual temple, saying, "My name, My eyes and My heart will rest upon them perpetually" (1 Pet. 2:5).

Eight "Power Points" in Solomon's Prayer

Eight incredible "power points" are revealed in this second prayer Solomon prayed. Let's take a look at each.

Power point #1

> Lord God of Israel, there is no God in heaven or on earth like You, who keep Your covenant and mercy with Your servants who walk before You with all their hearts.
>
> —2 Chronicles 6:14

In his prayer Solomon declared the uniqueness of the God of Israel. No man-made deity on earth can be compared to Him or offer what He offers: covenant and mercy.

A covenant is a binding agreement between two or more parties, each committing himself to fulfill certain obligations. God has established a total of nine major covenants in this world. God introduces the terms of a covenant, and it is up to human beings to accept those terms. If they do, God commits Himself to them.

One of the most powerful scriptures revealing the power of abiding in a covenant relationship with God was a prophecy given about David's dynasty by Jeremiah:

> Thus says the LORD: "If you can break My covenant with the day and My covenant with the night, so that there will not be day and night in their season, then My covenant may also be broken with David My servant, so that he shall not have a son to reign on his throne."
>
> —JEREMIAH 33:20–21

In other words, God was saying, "You will have to shut down the functions of the solar system before you can overthrow the dynasty of David." Our covenant with God is just as secure.

Mercy was the other unique attribute Solomon mentioned in his prayer. Mercy is compassion shown to offenders when judgment is deserved. David celebrated this attribute of God in Psalm 103:

> For as the heavens are high above the earth, so great is His mercy toward those who fear Him.
>
> —PSALM 103:11

> The mercy of the Lord is from everlasting to everlasting
> on those who fear Him…to such as keep His covenant.
> —Psalm 103:17–18

Though he backslid terribly, David was mercifully restored. That same mercy, demonstrated so powerfully in him, was passed on as a legacy to his house, preserving David's throne until the Messiah came (Jesus, the son of David). Then, when Jesus ascended to heaven, in a sense this King of all kings moved the throne of David to the highest and most glorious celestial realm. So God's promise that the throne of David would endure forever was fulfilled on a much higher level.

Similar promises have been given to us, such as the following:

> Therefore know that the Lord your God, He is God, the faithful God who keeps covenant and mercy for a thousand generations with those who love Him and keep His commandments.
> —Deuteronomy 7:9

How powerful is the mercy of the Lord! Blind Bartimaeus cried, "Jesus, Son of David, have mercy on me," and he received his sight (Mark 10:47). If a cry for mercy worked for him, surely it will work for us.

Action step: *Affirm to God that there is none like Him and that nothing can overthrow His covenant with you. Pray that He will pour out mercy on you and your house.*

Power point #2

> You have kept what You promised Your servant David my father; You have both spoken with Your mouth and fulfilled it with Your hand, as it is this day.

> Therefore, LORD God of Israel, now keep what You promised Your servant David my father, saying, "You shall not fail to have a man sit before Me on the throne of Israel, only if your sons take heed to their way, that they walk in My law as you have walked before Me."
>
> And now, O LORD God of Israel, let Your word come true, which You have spoken to Your servant David.
>
> —2 CHRONICLES 6:15–17

Showing gratitude is a high virtue. Here Solomon gratefully acknowledges the fulfillment of a past promise. God had been faithful to his father, David, miraculously carrying him through dangers, persecutions, and disappointments to that promised divine appointment of reigning over all of Israel. God had also supernaturally given him the design of the temple "by the Spirit" (1 Chron. 28:11–12). So that "promise" was finally fulfilled as well.

Giving the Creator due credit is also a virtuous thing. Even though it was David who stored up the materials and Solomon who oversaw the actual construction, it was God who supernaturally empowered them both to do these things. So the credit for the building and completion of the temple was assigned to God. Only after Solomon had done this did he ask for something new, the fulfilling of another promise, the preservation of his own throne and dynasty.

In like manner we should never rush into God's presence asking Him for new things or the fulfillment of yet unfulfilled promises until we have gratefully acknowledged what He has already done. Furthermore, even if we have accomplished great things for the kingdom, we should—as Solomon did—assign all the credit to the Most High: the

One who gives us life and breath, a mind to think with, the revelation of His will, and the power to bring it to pass.

Action step: *Express gratitude for things God has already done for you. Give God credit for everything you have accomplished, recognizing Him as your true source. Then ask Him to let His Word (written and living promises) "come true" in your life.*

Power point #3

> But will God indeed dwell with men on the earth? Behold, heaven and the heaven of heavens cannot contain You. How much less this temple which I have built!
>
> Yet regard the prayer of Your servant and his supplication, O Lord my God, and listen to the cry and the prayer which Your servant is praying before You: that Your eyes may be open toward this temple day and night, toward the place where You said You would put Your name, that You may hear the prayer which Your servant makes toward this place.
>
>   —2 Chronicles 6:18–20

Solomon proclaims the exceptional greatness of God and how small his abilities and efforts are in comparison. In like manner you should celebrate God's greatness: His omniscience, omnipresence, and omnipotence, declaring that He knows everything, He is everywhere, and He has all power. Exalt how vastly superior His ability is compared to yours.

Solomon acknowledges that the temple is not great within itself; rather, it is a mere building made with hands, insignificant compared to how big God is. The temple is great only because it is a place in which to hallow God's name. For this reason, Solomon requests that God's "eyes and ears" be attentive to the prayers that are prayed there.

Action step: *Declare God's exceptional greatness and your own inability in comparison. Remind God that your heart is His new covenant temple, where His name is enshrined. Ask that God's eyes and ears be set on you.*

Power point #4

Hear from heaven Your dwelling place, and when You hear, forgive.

—2 Chronicles 6:21

To acknowledge the need for forgiveness and to exhibit faith for it are essential attitudes of the heart. David pleaded with God, "Hide Your face from my sins, and blot out all my iniquities" (Ps. 51:9). Blotters were used to soak up the ink on paper so that errors no longer existed. So when God "blots out" our iniquities, they no longer exist as far as He is concerned. It is comparable to deleting something on a computer then emptying the trash bin. It no longer exists.

Forgiven people attract the glory of God—for it is written that He pours out "the riches of His glory on the vessels of mercy"—those who are mercifully delivered from their past errors (Rom. 9:23, see also 1 John 1:9).

Action step: *Claim the scriptures that promise forgiveness. They are for you.*

Power point #5

Now therefore, Arise, O Lord God, to Your resting place…

—2 Chronicles 6:41

With this statement Solomon was inviting the true God to come and inhabit the temple with His glory—in the midst of a world that often ignores His commandments, rejects

His lordship, grieves His Spirit, and blasphemes His name. How impossible it would be for God to feel "at rest" among such darkened, self-willed souls! But Solomon is promising the opposite, pledging to God that He will be hallowed, respected, obeyed, and adored among them. In essence he was saying, "You can feel at home with us; You can be at rest among us. We honor You. We exalt You to the highest place. We value our relationship with You. We want it to be permanent. So God, arise to Your resting place."

Action step: *Offer your heart and life as God's eternal "resting place"—the spiritual house where He will be reverenced, loved, and praised in the midst of a world at enmity with Him.*

Power point #6

> You and the ark of Your strength...
> —2 CHRONICLES 6:41

Wherever the ark of the covenant resided, its presence imparted supernatural strength. Often battles were won against superior odds because the ark, God's symbolic throne on the earth, was present. Of course it wasn't the gold-overlaid acacia wood box that imparted such strength, but the spiritual reality exemplified by it.

Strangely at that time, "nothing was in the ark except the two tablets which Moses put there at Horeb" (2 Chron. 5:10). Apparently the Philistines had removed Aaron's rod that budded, the golden bowl full of manna, and the Book of the Law. Why didn't they take the tablets of stone also?

Could it be they wanted the heavenly bread and the longevity it might give? They wanted the powerful rod that could part bodies of water and cause a river to gush out of a rock. They wanted the revelation and understanding of what God had done in the past (the scroll containing the Torah). But they didn't want God's Ten Commandments regulating their behavior. They didn't want His handwriting on their lives, His lordship, His dominating influence, His moral boundaries. They wanted the benefits but not the responsibilities of connecting with God.

Conversely, to welcome the "ark of His strength" is to welcome the demands of a covenantal relationship. It is to invite His enthronement in your heart, to welcome His laws guiding your actions, His commandments ruling your choices, His moral boundaries dictating your ethics. Of course, that's what the new covenant is all about, because in this era the Most High promises, "I will put My law in their minds, and write it on their hearts" (Jer. 31:33). His fiery finger is still engraving His will internally in those who surrender. And remember, where the ark is, the glory of God rests.

Action step: *Offer your heart as God's throne. Welcome the "ark of the covenant" into your inner being; ask God to write His law in your heart. Invite His glory into your life!*

Power point #7

> Let Your priests, O LORD God, be clothed with salvation, and let Your saints rejoice in goodness.
>
> —2 CHRONICLES 6:41

The word *salvation* means "deliverance." So to be "clothed with salvation" is to be adorned with God's deliverance power physically, mentally, emotionally, and spiritually. God has promised to manifest salvation in every area of our being, if we walk with Him, for He is the "author of eternal salvation"

(Heb. 5:9). Under the new covenant all believers are priests. (See 1 Peter 2:5, 9.)

Saints are sanctified persons, choice individuals who have been cleansed from sin, set apart, and dedicated to God for His purposes. When we worship, we "flow together to the goodness of the LORD" (Jer. 31:12, KJV).

Action step: *Acknowledge that you are a priest of God and ask Him to clothe you with salvation. Make a commitment to live a saintly life and rejoice in God's goodness.*

Power point #8

> O LORD God, do not turn away the face of Your Anointed; remember the mercies of Your servant David.
>
>   —2 CHRONICLES 6:42

Solomon ends this chapter-long prayer by referring to himself as God's "Anointed"—a faith-filled affirmation. He was acknowledging before God, "You've poured on me the oil of Your Spirit to accomplish an ordained task. Since it is Your purpose and not my own devising, please grace me to gaze in Your direction and be received, for I am Yours. And as a servant I exist to fulfill Your will."

When Solomon asked God to "remember the mercies of your servant David," he could also have been referring to the ancient prophecy that God would mercifully preserve the house of David and keep the dynasty safe from generation to generation. This request drew one of the most amazing responses from the God of heaven to be found in Scripture.

We should make this promise an object of meditation because this same kind of mercy is promised to all believers. In Isaiah 55:3 God encourages us all to:

Incline your ear, and come to Me. Hear, and your soul shall live; and I will make an everlasting covenant with you—the sure mercies of David.

Action step: *Claim the "sure mercies of David" in your life.*

An Undeniable Healing

There are so many verbal keys to Solomon's prayer. In this chapter, however, instead of emphasizing words, let's focus on the physical position he assumed. The Scripture says he "stood before the altar of the Lord in the presence of all the assembly of Israel, and *spread out his hands.*" Then he ascended the platform in the outer court to lead the dedication prayer. At that point he "knelt down on his knees before all the assembly of Israel, and *spread out his hands toward heaven*" (2 Chron. 6:12–13, emphasis added).

First Solomon spread out his hands toward the place of atoning sacrifice on the earth; then he lifted his hands toward God's place of enthronement in the celestial sphere. He first acknowledged the source of cleansing and forgiveness; then he acknowledged the source of dominion and victory.

There is nothing "magical" about assuming certain physical postures in prayer (as some religions believe). It is not necessary to adopt a certain position for the cry of the heart to be heard. You can be walking, standing, sitting, kneeling, or prostrate on the floor. You can have your head bowed and your hands folded. Or you can have your head and hands lifted. None of these things are "sacred keys" that insure the answer we seek will come.

However, that being said, we still need to understand that the lifting of hands in worship is highly symbolic and, at times, even prophetic in nature. It is a prayer method the Word of God encourages. Whenever God's people raise their hands to Him in adoration, a powerful statement is being made in the Spirit.

Consider the following scriptures:

> Let us lift up our heart with our hands unto God in the heavens.
> —LAMENTATIONS 3:41, KJV

> My hands also I will lift up to Your commandments, which I love.
> —PSALM 119:48

> Let my prayer be set before You as incense, the lifting up of my hands as the evening sacrifice.
> —PSALM 141:2

> I spread out my hands to you; my soul longs for you like a thirsty land. Selah
> —PSALM 143:6

> I desire therefore that the men pray everywhere, lifting up holy hands, without wrath and doubting.
> —1 TIMOTHY 2:8

So the lifting of hands is a method of worshipping God that is encouraged and commanded in the Bible. On the basis of the scriptures just quoted, when believers lift their hands in prayer and praise they are really:

- Lifting their hearts up to God
- Expressing love for, and submission to, His commandments

+ Offering themselves as a burnt sacrifice to God: on fire with desire and consecrated wholly to Him (the "evening sacrifice" was a burnt offering)

+ Expressing a deep, soul-penetrating thirst for communion with God

+ Banishing wrath (no longer harboring anger, bitterness, or unforgiveness toward God or people)

+ Exiling unbelief and entering God's gates instead with faith and trust

In the light of these passages it is easy to see what a powerful prophetic statement is being made "in the Spirit" when we assume this posture toward the Most High.

The most powerful example of the effectiveness of lifting hands to God that I have ever witnessed involved a woman who came to one of my healing services with a very serious, medically documented case of multiple sclerosis (MS). In the summer of 1993 Karen arrived at Strawberry Lake Christian Retreat in Ogema, Minnesota, hoping only for a spiritual impartation. At the age of thirty-three she had been sick for ten years and diagnosed for four. The doctors had labeled her permanently disabled. She had given birth to a baby girl a year before but had not been able to even stand up and hold the newborn child in her arms. Every morning her husband, Dave, had to carry the baby downstairs, then carry Karen downstairs before leaving for work.

The night she came to my meeting she could barely walk, even with the help of a cane and the steadying hands of those with her. Strangely she was not charismatic and did not believe in healing. Still, she responded to the altar call and knelt down, pouring out her heart to God and praying for His mercy. She was not even asking for a miracle.

Seeing her sincerity, I asked Karen to stand up and lift her hands in praise (unknown to me, she had never done that before). I lifted my hands toward heaven as well, and we began worshipping together with tears flowing down both our faces. The glory of God rushed in the room. Everyone sensed it. Karen told me, "That's when I felt the Holy Spirit blow through me three times, and I was filled with faith and hope." Feeling an assurance, I shouted, "Sister, I believe you are healed!"

She walked around the church that night without the help of her cane while we all shouted. When the sun rose the next morning, everything had changed dramatically. Her two sons got so excited they started jumping up and down on the bed. With newfound strength surging through her body, Karen picked up her baby girl, Johanna, and walked about a half-mile to the lakefront (an absolutely impossible task prior to her miracle).

When her husband drove up to Strawberry Lake later that day, he was in shock, unable to believe his own eyes. However, convinced of God's reality, Dave ended up getting saved about two weeks later. Both sons were saved. Six months later Dave quit his job, the family sold their possessions, and they took off for ministry school. It's been many years now and Karen is still completely delivered.

Would Karen have been healed without lifting her hands that night? Only God knows the answer to that question. Surely it wasn't a necessary prerequisite—but that's the way it happened. Surely it wasn't a requirement for Solomon to lift his hands either. But he did. And the glory came. As I am writing these words, I feel compelled to lift my hands and shout in faith, "God, send Your glory again!"

What About You?

Now it is time for you to pray, confess, and believe the power points in the Solomon temple prayer. The following bulleted statements summarize what we have covered in this chapter. After reviewing these points, create your own prayer. Use as many parts of Solomon's prayer as you can, especially the eight points specified.

+ Affirm that there is no god like your God.
+ Praise Him in full expectation that He will keep His covenant.
+ Ask God to pour out mercy on you and your household.
+ Express gratitude for things God has already done.
+ Give God credit for everything you have accomplished, acknowledging Him as your source.
+ Declare God's exceptional greatness and your own inability in comparison.
+ Remind God that you are His new covenant temple.
+ Celebrate before God that His name is enshrined in your heart.
+ Ask God to set His eyes and ears on you and answer your prayers.

+ Claim forgiveness. Offer your heart as God's place of rest.

+ Offer your heart as a throne for the almighty God.

+ Offer your heart as a container for the ark of the covenant, in a spiritual sense.

+ Invite God to write His commandments and promises with His fiery finger in every area of your being.

+ Invite God's glory into your life.

+ Confess that you are a priest and ask God to clothe you with salvation.

+ Confess that you are one of God's saints, cleansed from sin and set apart for a holy purpose.

+ Rejoice in God's goodness.

+ Ask God to pour out the sure mercies of David in your life.

Now it's your turn to pray:

Lord God of Solomon, [compose your prayer as the Holy Spirit leads, using the bullet points above as needed].

Chapter 5

THE PRAYER OF ASA

Lord, it is nothing for You to help...
2 Chronicles 14:11

A SA WAS THE third king of Judah. His grandfather Rehoboam was the immature and belligerent monarch who inherited the throne from his father, Solomon. Recklessly acting on the wrong advice from young counselors, Rehoboam caused a rift in Israel and ten tribes seceded to the north.

However, Rehoboam's grandson Asa grew up to be a wise man. He was also passionate for the things of God, removing idolatry from the land and even deposing his own grandmother because of her false religious practices. In his days Judah "entered into a covenant to seek the Lord God of their fathers with all their heart and with all their soul" (2 Chron. 15:12). During Asa's reign the land of Judah also enjoyed a time of rest from all their enemies round about.

When Asa prayed the words quoted at the beginning of this chapter, the largest army ever to invade the southern kingdom of Judah was approaching its borders—a military juggernaut of around a million soldiers that intended to seize the nation. Disaster seemed imminent, a bloodbath that would rout the people of God out of their inheritance.

But Asa sought the Lord and God intervened supernaturally. Here is the concise biblical account:

> Then Zerah the Ethiopian came out against them with an army of a million men and three hundred chariots, and he came to Mareshah. So Asa went out against him, and they set the troops in battle array in the Valley of Zephathah at Mareshah. And Asa cried out to the LORD his God, and said: *"LORD, it is nothing for You to help, whether with many or with those who have no power; help us, O LORD our God, for we rest on You, and in Your name we go against this multitude. O LORD, You are our God; do not let man prevail against You!"*
>
> So the LORD struck the Ethiopians before Asa and Judah, and the Ethiopians fled. And Asa and the people who were with him pursued them to Gerar. So the Ethiopians were overthrown, and they could not recover, for they were broken before the LORD and His army. And they carried away very much spoil. Then they defeated all the cities around Gerar, for the fear of the LORD came upon them; and they plundered all the cities, for there was exceedingly much spoil in them.
>
> —2 CHRONICLES 14:9–14, EMPHASIS ADDED

Asa's army was about half the size of its foes. It was comprised of three hundred thousand men of Judah "who carried shields and spears," and two hundred eighty thousand men of Benjamin "who carried shields and drew bows"—"all of these were mighty men of valor" (2 Chron. 14:8). The odds were against them (about two-to-one), but God was with them—and that made all the difference.

God's Supernatural Response

One of the most remarkable attributes of Asa's prayer is its brevity. Quote it with a timer. It takes only about twenty seconds. Yet it changed the course of a nation. Its power hinged not on the quantity of words spoken but the quality. They were saturated with faith, the very thing that pleases God.

Charles Spurgeon said it so well, "True prayer is measured by weight, not by length. A single groan before God may have more fullness of prayer in it than a fine oration of great length."[1] Because one man dared to minimize his problem and maximize God's power, a heathen army was conquered and Judah was saved from destruction. You see, battles are often won spiritually before they are ever faced naturally.

The Bible doesn't tell us many details of how the victory was secured for the armies of Judah that day. It merely shares the following:

> So the LORD struck the Ethiopians before Asa and Judah, and the Ethiopians fled. And Asa and the people who were with him pursued them to Gerar. So the Ethiopians were overthrown, and they could not recover, for they were broken before the LORD and His army. And they carried away very much spoil.
>
> —2 CHRONICLES 14:12–13

On the basis of these two verses, if we pray the way Asa prayed, we should expect God to supernaturally strike our adversaries (the demonic forces that war against us). They should reel under the impact to such a degree that in a similar way they will "not recover," but instead be "broken before the Lord." At the end of the day, like Judah, if we dare to believe we will walk away with "much spoil." God will make the attack of the enemy to work in our favor.

Six "Power-Points" in Asa's Prayer

There are six "power points" revealed in Asa's prayer. Let's look at each carefully.

Power point #1

> Lord, it is nothing for You to help…
>
> —2 Chronicles 14:11

At the very beginning of this prayer Asa dared to use the word "nothing." He was boasting that the immense challenge he was facing was no challenge at all to God. Quite possibly, Asa was measuring the possibility of an earthly miracle by the immeasurable vastness of the cosmos and heavenly worlds beyond. Our trials and tests are infinitesimally small when contrasted with the impossible conditions God faced in the beginning—formlessness, emptiness, and void. Yet "nothingness" bowed to His authority! Creation burst into being at the sound of His voice. (See Genesis 1.)

What should our conclusion be? If God can create all things out of "nothing," then it is "nothing" for Him to intervene in the most difficult circumstances. No wonder Jeremiah shouted, "Ah, Lord God! Behold, You have made the heavens and the earth by Your great power and outstretched arm. *There is nothing too hard for You*" (Jer. 32:17, emphasis added).

Action step: *Declare that your situation is "nothing" for God to handle.*

Power point #2

Whether with many or with those who have no power...
—2 Chronicles 14:11

First Asa reminded God that He has all power; then he informed God that He is not hindered by those who have "no power." How opposite this is compared with what we think is necessary to exhibit faith. However, God does not need us to boast in our own abilities or even our God-given abilities. Those who are fighting for His cause may be "unlearned and ignorant" (Acts 4:13, kjv) by the world's standards and yet be used of God mightily to fulfill His purposes.

Pastor and author W. S. Bowd revealed, "Prayer is weakness leaning on omnipotence."[2] It is not a "negative self-image" that would cause us to acknowledge our bankruptcy in Adam or to declare our utter dependence on God. To do so does not indicate weak faith. On the contrary, only those who admit, "Without Him I can do nothing" (see John 15:5) can rightfully go on to assert, "I can do all things through Christ who strengthens me" (Phil. 4:13). Only those who concede their human deficiency can successfully tap into their divine sufficiency.

Asa was doing this; he was admitting, "God You don't really need us, but we need You. The size of our army is irrelevant. Our training and experience add nothing to Your ability. We are totally dependent upon Your power."

When he approached God with that "poor in spirit" attitude, it was like a limp, disconnected, powerless electric cord getting plugged into a hot socket and the lights coming on. God came through mightily because He was acknowledged as the source of help. Many years later Zechariah enshrined this concept in an often-quoted prophecy:

> "Not by might nor by power, but by My Spirit," says the Lord of hosts.
>
> —Zechariah 4:6

How profoundly God unveiled this concept to Paul in a time of struggle, saying: "My grace is sufficient for you, for My strength is made perfect in weakness." This caused the apostle to conclude, "I will rather boast in my infirmities, that the power of Christ may rest upon me....For when I am weak, then I am strong" (2 Cor. 12:9–10). What a mystery this is!

Action step: *Admit your own inadequacy and declare total trust in God's adequacy.*

Power point #3

> Help us, O Lord our God, for we rest on You.
>
> —2 Chronicles 14:11

What does it mean to rest on God? It means to have abiding in faith, calmly praising God for victory in advance and not allowing nervous anxiety to take over our emotions and thoughts. Psalm 37:7 says, "Rest in the Lord, and wait patiently for Him." Hebrews 4:3 adds, "We who have believed do enter that rest." For a king to declare his nation was "resting" on God as an enemy army twice their size marched their direction was no small matter. That took nerves of steel. It is not an easy-to-fulfill mandate for us either, yet the Bible does say, "Be anxious for nothing" (Phil. 4:6).

Action step: *Affirm that you refuse to be anxious and instead intend to rest in God and rest your faith on His Word.*

Power point #4

And in Your name we go against this multitude.

—2 Chronicles 14:11

To do something "in the name of the Lord" is to do it by His power, through His authority, as His representatives, and for His glory. A great way to pray "in His name" is to declare the various unique names of God, then praise Him for the unique manifestation of what each name means. As you seek God in prayer, you should make declarations such as the following:

I rise up in faith against this adversity in the name of:

El Shaddai, God Almighty, who is mightier than all my foes (Gen. 17:1)

El Gibbor, the Mighty God, who strengthens me with might in my inner man (Isa. 9:1–7)

El Elyon, God Most High, who is higher than the highest principalities that oppose me (Gen. 14:18)

El Roi, the God who sees, for He "sees" the deepest part of my heart, and all the battles of my life (Gen. 16:8–13)

Yahweh M'Kaddesh, the God who sanctifies, who cleanses me and sets me apart to fulfill His purposes (Exod. 31:13)

Yahweh-Nissi, the Lord my Banner, who goes before me in battle and is the cause for which I fight (Exod. 17:15)

Yahweh-Rohi, the Lord my Shepherd, who leads me beside still waters of purpose and makes me lie down in green pastures of abundance (Ps. 23)

Yahweh-Rophe, the Lord my Healer, who heals me in every part of my being (Exod. 15:26)

Yahweh-Shalom, the Lord my Peace, who gives me peace in the midst of the storm (Judg. 6:24)

Yahweh-Tsidkenu, the Lord my Righteousness, who grants me a status of righteousness in His sight (Jer. 23:6)

Yahweh-Tsebaoth, the Lord of Hosts, the God of an army of angels, who are commissioned to defend me and remain poised and ready for battle (1 Sam. 1:3)

Yes, I come against this adversity in the name that is above every name, the name of Jesus the Messiah (Yeshua Mashiach). I confess that because the name Jesus *means the "salvation of God" and* Messiah *means the "Anointed One," that according to Hebrews 7:25 and Isaiah 10:27 my God will save me to the uttermost and His anointing will break every yoke in my life.*

Amen and amen!

Action step: *Declare the names of God over your situation and apply their meaning.*

Power point #5

O Lord, You are our God.

—2 Chronicles 14:11

The use of the possessive pronoun "our" was Asa's way of confidently saying, "You are not the God of these Ethiopians who are attacking us. You are the God of Israel. We are in a special relationship with You." So the odds were on the side of God's people. As Paul said many centuries later, "If God is for us, who can be against us?" (Rom. 8:31).

Action step: *Declare that you have a special relationship with the true God.*

Power point #6

> Do not let man prevail against You!
> —2 Chronicles 14:11

This is a prayerful invitation for God to own the battle. King Asa was making it clear, "If they come against us, they are actually coming against You, God. And if they prevail against us, they have prevailed against You." Such a daring way of throwing the responsibility on God was reminiscent of King David's faith, when he ran toward the giant Goliath shouting, "The battle is the Lord's, and He will give you into our hands!" (1 Sam. 17:47).

Action step: *Invite God to own your battle and vindicate Himself by defeating the enemies in your life.*

Conquering Lightning

Back in 1989 I was conducting a tent meeting just off State Road 74 in Monroe, North Carolina. One night a terrible lightning storm swept through the region, spawned by Hurricane Hugo. About fifty die-hard believers came out to the tent meeting anyway, defying "mother nature" in the name of the Lord. The wind was blowing furiously, causing the top of the big tent to balloon up dangerously. While the people were straining to hear my message above the roar of the heavy downpour, they simultaneously had to dodge quarter poles swinging from side to side in the air.

Everyone was getting sprayed; the curtains kept billowing up from the fierce winds, and sheets of rain were diffusing through the tent. The ropes connected to the stakes were pulling so tight they appeared on the verge of snapping at any moment. Earlier that day we had even placed twenty-five-foot-long telephone poles between the first and second rows of stakes to help prevent them from being pulled up.

I kept trying to encourage the people with faith-filled statements such as, "You're in the safest place in town *because God's here!* You're safer here than you would be in a brick building!" It was all quite unnerving and intense, but we all had the mind-set that nothing would deter us.

Back then cordless microphones were not commonly used, so with my right hand I was tightly gripping a mike attached to a fifty-foot cable connected to the amplifier that was plugged directly into the power outlet. Suddenly lightning struck one of the three tall center poles holding the tent up. The sound was nearly deafening. The air crackled, electrified.

Unfortunately I was the closest person to the pole. A "flash of fire" struck me in the right hand (apparently there was an attraction to the metal microphone). I lit up (there are witnesses to this day who will verify this). The jolt knocked the mike about thirty feet out of my hand as the surge of power went through my body and into the ground.

I was totally stunned, unable to speak, hardly able to gather my thoughts. For a moment I couldn't fathom who I was, where I was, or why those fifty people were gazing at me so incredulously. Little by little it all returned. I even remembered where

I left off in my sermon. So I started preaching again at that same point. The look of awe on the faces of those who saw the incident increased when I said, "That should have killed me."

That's when a young woman who was physically challenged struggled to run up to me. As I remember, she was the daughter of one of our supporting pastors. She blurted out, "Preacher, if you can endure a lightning blast, you can pray the prayer of faith for me." Still fuzzy in my mind (which is an understatement), I felt like saying, "Young lady, I'm the one in need of prayer right now."

Instead, I tried my best to listen intently as she described her condition. Severe scoliosis in her spine had twisted her body and wracked her with extreme pain for years (you could even see the bones protruding from under her blouse). Furthermore, one of her legs was about an inch and a half shorter than the other, making it necessary for her to wear a specially made shoe.

We probably had two different reasons for expecting a miracle that night, similar to two different aspects of Asa's prayer.

+ She was thinking (in Asa-like manner), "If God can spare this minister from what should have killed him, it is *nothing* for Him to fix my body."

+ I was thinking (in Asa-like manner), "Lord, if You do this, *it will have to be You*, because I feel totally incapable right now. I'm barely able to think, much less pray."

She was declaring God's omnipotence; I was declaring my spiritual impotence. But as feeble as my efforts were, my faith and her faith were both in God and in the promise of

His Word. We were in total agreement, claiming Matthew 18:18–19:

> Assuredly, I say to you, whatever you bind on earth will be bound in heaven, and whatever you loose on earth will be loosed in heaven.
>
> Again I say to you that if two of you agree on earth concerning anything that they ask, it will be done for them by My Father in heaven.

I never got to even touch her forehead. While I was still stretching forth my hand and speaking the name of Jesus, the power of God hit her so forcefully that she shook and quaked from one end of the tent to the other. When she came out from under the power of the Holy Spirit, every vertebra in her back had straightened. Then, as we prayed over her leg, the shorter one grew out to its perfect length. In fact, she had to take off her shoes in order to walk back to her seat because the old elevated shoe caused her to tip over and lose her balance.

I have always considered that creative miracle to be one of the greatest manifestations I have ever witnessed in one of my meetings. But I must admit, that night I prayed right before falling asleep, "Father, I really appreciate Your working such a powerful miracle tonight, but if You don't mind, please build the people's faith from now on just by the preaching of the Word." I think He probably smiled when He heard me say that.

What About You?

Now it is time for you to pray, confess, and believe the power points in the Asa prayer. The following bulleted statements summarize what we have covered in this chapter. After reviewing these points, create your own prayer. Use as many parts of the Asa prayer as you can, especially the six points specified.

+ Inform the Lord it is nothing for Him to change your situation.
+ Remind God of your utter dependency on Him, that you have no might within yourself.
+ Declare God's omnipotence, that He possesses *all* power.
+ Confess Zechariah 4:6, "'Not by might nor by power, but by My Spirit,' says the Lord of hosts."
+ Refuse to be anxious.
+ Affirm that you are "resting" on God.
+ Celebrate the names of God, applying their revelation to your situation.
+ Remind God of the special relationship you enjoy with Him.
+ Appeal to God to own your battle, and not to let the enemy of your soul prevail against Him.

Now it's your turn to pray:

Lord God of Asa, [compose your prayer as the Holy Spirit leads, using the bullet points above as needed].

Chapter 6

THE PRAYER OF JEHOSHAPHAT

O Lord God of our fathers, are You not God in heaven?
2 Chronicles 20:6

King Jehoshaphat was the son of righteous King Asa, who was part of the dynasty of David. He inherited the throne in 914 BC at the age of thirty-five. For twenty-five years he reigned over Judah (the name for the southern kingdom, which was actually made of up two tribes: Judah and Benjamin). The name *Jehoshaphat* means "the Lord is judge."[1] He is celebrated in biblical history as being one of the most pious kings to reign over God's people. He was zealous for true religion, a lover of the Torah (the law), passionate about seeking God, and inspiring in his ability to believe and act upon the prophetic word of the Lord.

For years Jehoshaphat strengthened the Jews against the northern kingdom of Israel, which was made up of the ten tribes that broke away from the rule of the Davidic dynasty. They were a serious threat to Judah, both militarily and spiritually, because they were larger in number and because they were steeped in false religion.

However, an even greater peril surfaced when three Gentile kings with massive armies united to attack Judah: the Ammonites, the Moabites, and the dwellers in Mount Seir. It looked like destruction was imminent, but Jehoshaphat took a bold step of faith. The Scripture says he "feared, and set himself to seek the LORD" (2 Chron. 20:3).

The Scripture goes on to say:

> Then Jehoshaphat stood in the assembly of Judah and Jerusalem, in the house of the LORD, before the new court, and said: *"O LORD God of our fathers, are You not God in heaven, and do You not rule over all the kingdoms of the nations, and in Your hand is there not power and might, so that no one is able to withstand You? Are You not our God, who drove out the inhabitants of this land before Your people Israel, and gave it to the descendants of Abraham Your friend forever? And they dwell in it, and have built You a sanctuary in it for Your name, saying, 'If disaster comes upon us—sword, judgment, pestilence, or famine—we will stand before this temple and in Your presence (for Your name is in this temple), and cry out to You in our affliction, and You will hear and save.' And now, here are the people of Ammon, Moab, and Mount Seir—whom You would not let Israel invade when they came out of the land of Egypt, but they turned from them and did not destroy them—here they are, rewarding us by coming to throw us out of Your possession which You have given us to inherit. O our God, will You not judge them? For we have no power against this great multitude that is coming against us; nor do we know what to do, but our eyes are upon You."*
>
> —2 CHRONICLES 20:5–12, EMPHASIS ADDED

Jehoshaphat declared that His eyes were on the Lord—and that made all the difference.

God's Supernatural Response

Before we look at what God did in response to Jehoshaphat's prayer, I want to look briefly at the way this notable king demonstrated his faith in God. The Scripture explains that after King Jehoshaphat prayed this prayer, "Judah...stood before the LORD" (2 Chron. 20:13). They were in a receptive mode, waiting on God. Then the Spirit of God moved on one of the sons of Asaph, a Levite named Jahaziel, who gave the most astounding prophecy:

> Listen, all you of Judah and you inhabitants of Jerusalem, and you, King Jehoshaphat! Thus says the LORD to you: "Do not be afraid nor dismayed because of this great multitude, for the battle is not yours, but God's.... You will not need to fight in this battle. Position yourselves, stand still and see the salvation of the LORD, who is with you, O Judah and Jerusalem!" Do not fear or be dismayed; tomorrow go out against them, for the LORD is with you.
> —2 CHRONICLES 20:15, 17

At that pivotal moment Jehoshaphat believed God was able. It is important to notice exactly how he acted on his faith in God's ability to deliver them. First, Jehoshaphat awakened faith by boldly declaring to the Jews, "Believe in the LORD your God, and you shall be established; believe His prophets, and you shall prosper" (2 Chron. 20:20). Look closely at the Scripture reference. I call it the Bible's "20/20 vision" passage—the key to perfect, spiritual vision.

The next thing Jehoshaphat did was send his soldiers out on the battlefield without any weapons (*gulp!*). They became radical faith-fighters and spiritual warriors: playing instruments of music and singing, "Praise the LORD, for His mercy endures forever" (2 Chron. 20:21). Praise is one of the most powerful forms that faith can take. To praise God in advance for a breakthrough is to seize it with full confidence.

What a tactic! What psychological warfare! Surely the enemy soldiers were bewildered, wondering what these Jews were up to. Then it happened: the supernatural intervention that shocked everyone.

The Bible doesn't explain exactly how God delivered the people. It simply says "the LORD set ambushes against the people of Ammon, Moab, and Mount Seir...and they were defeated" (2 Chron. 20:22). Though we are not given the details, it seems the enemies of the Jews were "ambushed" by bands of angels who created chaos within their ranks. Apparently they injected such confusion into the battle that the enemies of Israel began slaughtering one another. In a very short time they were all destroyed.

The Jews spent the next three days gathering all the spoil! For that reason, they renamed that location the Valley of Berachah ("the valley of blessing") for in that place they were "blessed" beyond measure and in that place they "blessed" the Lord (2 Chron. 20:23–27). What looked like utter defeat became a source of great prosperity! What looked like a curse in the end became a blessing!

Ten "Power Points" in Jehoshaphat's Prayer

There are ten "power points" in the prayer of Jehoshaphat. Let's examine each.

Power point #1

O, Lord God of our fathers...

—2 Chronicles 20:6

From the start of his prayer Jehoshaphat reminded God of the historical relationship the Israelites possessed with the God of their forefathers Abraham, Isaac, and Jacob. The continuation of this relationship was expected from generation to generation because this was understood to be the Lord's normal pattern. He later revealed this "generational" commitment through Isaiah, saying, "I will pour My Spirit on your descendants, and My blessing on your offspring" (Isa. 44:3).

Action step: *Remind God of His former commitments to the patriarchs Abraham, Isaac, and Jacob, and that you too can trace roots back to them because those who are "of faith" are "the children of Abraham" (Gal. 3:7, KJV).*

Power point #2

Are You not God in heaven?

—2 Chronicles 20:6

As far as we know, the third heaven (paradise) is the highest realm in the universe, and God is the highest authority in that realm. So Jehoshaphat establishes the God of Israel as the "Most High" (Ps. 91:1). If He truly is "God" in the highest celestial world, then He is certainly "God" in this inferior world below.

Action step: *Declare God's dominion in heaven.*

Power point #3

> And do You not rule over all the kingdoms of the nations?
> —2 Chronicles 20:6

A kingdom is a king's domain. Every king wields absolute authority over his kingdom. No major decisions that affect the kingdom can be made without the king's agreement. So Jehoshaphat asserted that God is actually the King of kings. Though earthly monarchs "appear" to be sovereign, they are not. God can cancel out their decisions any time He chooses.

Action step: *Declare God's authority in the earth.*

Power point #4

> In Your hand is there not power and might, so that no one is able to withstand You?
> —2 Chronicles 20:6

Jehoshaphat once again clarified that God already possesses all necessary power (the word *power* means both "authority" and "ability") to conquer the enemy. Years before, David wrote, "God has spoken once, twice I have heard this: that power belongs to God" (Ps. 62:11). Therefore, He can effortlessly overthrow any earthly thing that dares to resist His will.

Action step: *Declare God's absolute power and the enemy's utter weakness.*

Power point #5

> Are You not our God…?
> —2 Chronicles 20:7

Jehoshaphat again acknowledged the special relationship the Jews enjoyed with the Creator. He is not just "God" in a general sense; He is "their God" in a personal and committed sense. That speaks of covenant relationship, a sharing of burdens and battles. To say, "Are You not our God" is a way of saying, "We belong to You. Therefore, our battles are Your battles."

Action step: *Affirm your covenant connection with God.*

Power point #6

> Who drove out the inhabitants of this land before Your people Israel…
>
> —2 Chronicles 20:7

How powerful it is to rehearse before God something He has already supernaturally accomplished in the past! Doing so raises the bar of expectation that He will do it again—or something of similar magnitude.

As we lift this account from 2 Chronicles 20 to a new covenant application, the identity of the "enemy" changes drastically. Just as God empowered the Israelites to drive the Canaanites out of their "physical" Promised Land, so He empowers us to drive demonic forces out of our "spiritual" land of promise. This is not a natural land; rather, it is a "supernatural" land comprised of two things:

1. All the promises God has given in His written Word (a total of 7,487).[2]

2. All the living Word promises He has given us personally.

After salvation evil spirits often attempt to invade our lives again in order to block the fulfillment of God's promises. However, just as Jehoshaphat did, we can reaffirm God's past actions toward us and drive the enemy out again in the name of the Lord.

Action step: *Rehearse God's former victories and declare His promises (both written Word promises and promises God has spoken to you personally).*

Power point #7

> And gave it to the descendants of Abraham Your friend forever?
> —2 CHRONICLES 20:7

It is also effective to remind God of commitments He has already made, because as far as He is concerned, those promises are a "done deal." Jehoshaphat brought to God's remembrance the commitment He made many times before. For instance, right after Lot split off and settled in the plains of Sodom, God spoke to his uncle Abraham, saying, "Lift your eyes now and look from the place where you are—northward, southward, eastward, and westward; for all the land which you see I give to you and your descendants forever" (Gen. 13:14–15). This wasn't just a future hope; it was a past tense fact. The land belonged to them—period.

Nevertheless, whenever you find God making a pledge, you also find the enemy attempting to counteract the pledge to render it null and void. Surely that's why Jesus warned, "The kingdom of heaven suffers violence, and the violent take it by force" (Matt. 11:12). God-anointed prayer warriors must be forceful—violent in faith—in order to successfully seize God's promises and see them fulfilled. We must, like Jehoshaphat, have the mind-set that these things *already* belong to us—"as His divine power has given to us all things that pertain to life and godliness" (2 Pet. 1:3). Then we will pray as if peace, joy, righteousness, strength, healing, and deliverance are *already* credited to our accounts.

Action step: *Prophesy your inheritance rights!*

Power point #8

> And they dwell in it, and have built You a sanctuary in it for Your name, saying, "If disaster comes upon us—sword, judgment, pestilence, or famine—we will stand before this temple and in Your presence (for Your name is in this temple), and cry out to You in our affliction, and You will hear and save."
>
> —2 Chronicles 20:8–9

Wherever you find God's temple, you also find His presence and His name. And where you find these three things, you find prayers being answered and salvation manifesting. If this was true when God's habitation was a lifeless building, how much truer it is now! We are His living temple. His presence and His name dwell within our regenerated hearts.

Action step: *Affirm that you are God's temple and that God's name abides in you.*

Power point #9

> And now, here are the people of Ammon, Moab, and Mount Seir—whom You would not let Israel invade when they came out of the land of Egypt, but they turned from them and did not destroy them—here they are, rewarding

us by coming to throw us out of Your possession which
You have given us to inherit. O our God, will You not
judge them?

$\qquad$—2 Chronicles 20:10–12

We should identify the things that are sent to rob us of
our inheritance and then invite God to "judge" our situation
and execute "judgment" against our enemies (satanic forces)
that come to "steal, and to kill, and to destroy" (John 10:10).

Notice in this part of the prayer, Jehoshaphat also declared
the land of promise was not just their "inheritance" from
the Lord; it was also God's "possession." In like manner, we
should remind our heavenly Father, "What's mine is Yours,
Lord—my home, my family, my possessions, my calling, my
purpose, my mind, my body—so I pray You will defend what
actually belongs to you!"

Action step: *Identify enemy activity and entreat God to judge and
counterattack.*

Power point #10

For we have no power against this great multitude that is
coming against us, nor do we know what to do, but our
eyes are upon You.

$\qquad$—2 Chronicles 20:12

It is not detrimental to faith to acknowledge weakness in
the face of a problem as long as we acknowledge our source
of superior strength—the expectation that God will take up
the slack and make up the difference. Even when you are
unsure what step to take next, you can affirm your absolute
trust in God by saying, "My eyes are upon You."

In other words, you are saying, "Lord, I may not know

what to do, but You know, and I am looking to You for guidance and for a miracle of divine deliverance. Even when the odds appear to be against me, I believe God that You are on my side, so I expect to overcome."

Action step: *Be willing to admit your inadequacy and trust in God's adequacy. Tell God you are not looking at your circumstance; your eyes are on Him.*

My "Valley of Blessing"

Back in the 1970s and 1980s, I used to conduct tent crusades throughout the United States on a shoestring budget (more like a worn-out flip-flop budget—there were no shoestrings). In the beginning, I transported a sixty-foot by one-hundred-twenty-foot tent in an old, dilapidated school bus. With a thirty-foot platform, three hundred chairs, metal center poles and quarter poles, and over one hundred half-axle stakes, the bus was overloaded.

On the way to Tampa, Florida, one year we hit a pothole in the road so hard that it dented the rim of one of the rear wheels. Because a slight stream of air began slowly escaping, every forty miles or so we had to stop and pump up the nearly bald tire again and again. Once I got to Tampa I decided to visit the junkyards to see if I could get two used rims (one to replace the damaged rim and another for a spare).

Much to my surprise, everywhere I went, all the old junk-yard cronies informed me, "You won't find those rims any-where in town. They phased out those old split rims years ago because they were so dangerous. Many people got injured. We melted them all down as scrap metal." And they were right. I never could find a match for my bus. Two-and-a-half weeks later I had to go to my next meeting in Bessemer City, North Carolina, knowing I would have to use a seriously handicapped vehicle. But like Jehoshaphat's soldiers stepping on the battlefield, I made the decision to get on the highway anyway.

The trip took an enormous amount of time because we had to stop every hour. My "battlefield" was a six hundred-mile stretch of interstate highway. But the whole way I worshipped God, reminding Him there was nothing we could do to fix the situation, claiming angelic protection, and praising God for getting us all the way there. Though I didn't implement all the elements of the Jehoshaphat prayer, I used some of the most important parts.

You should have seen the look of astonishment on our faces when we finally pulled onto the lot in Bessemer City! There they were, right in the middle of the tent lot: two big, nearly new truck tires, exactly the size I needed, mounted on split rims, exactly the type I used. Incredible! We were awestruck. The odds of that happening are incalculable. It may have transpired naturally (maybe the circus occupying the lot before us left them in the field). Or God may have done it supernaturally (He could have just created them). Regardless, it was a miracle.

In a sense we passed through an emotionally charged "valley" of a negative circumstance, but it became for us a "Valley of Berachah" (a valley of blessing) because we definitely ended up being "blessed" and we definitely ended up blessing the Lord (2 Chron. 20:26).

Did it happen because I prayed to the "Lord of hosts" (the God of an army of angels that are poised and ready for battle) and claimed the protection of those ministering spirits? Did it happen because, like Jehoshaphat's soldiers, we praised God in advance for the victory all the way to North Carolina? Yes, I believe it all hinged on our prayerfulness and intercession.

Though the "tire miracle" alone was enough to send our spirits soaring, something else transpired later that day that added greatly to our awareness that God was in the arrangements. As we were putting up the tent, a white dove walked out of an adjoining wooded area and allowed itself to be caught. Again, we had no idea if it had been owned by someone in the circus before us or if God had simply sent it to us, but for several days before the meeting we let that dove fly around inside the tent. From the first night our meeting was packed, with many drunks and drug users finding the Lord. The hand of the Lord moved mightily in an unforgettable way. *For the Lord is good, and His mercy endures forever.* (See Psalm 100:5; 2 Chronicles 20:21.)

What About You?

Now it is time for you to pray, confess, and believe the power points in the Jehoshaphat prayer. The following bulleted statements summarize what we have learned in this chapter. After rehearsing these points, create your own prayer. Use as many parts of Jehoshaphat's prayer as you can, especially the ten points specified:

+ Declare that because of your faith you are a child of Abraham and you are an heir to the blessings he received.

+ Declare God's supremacy, authority, power, and dominion.

+ Remind God of supernatural things He has already done for you in the past.

+ Rehearse promises He has already made to you (in the written Word or personal living word promises).

+ Announce that you are God's temple and that the name of the Lord resides in you.

+ Identify what the enemy is attempting to do.

+ Remind God that the satanic agenda against you is trespassing into the inheritance He has given you.

+ Invite God to be the "judge" between you and your spiritual adversaries.

+ Admit your helplessness in the flesh (to dethrone spiritual pride).

+ Assert the fact that your "eyes" are upon the Lord (to enthrone faith).

+ Speak prophetically that "the battle is the Lord's."

+ Celebrate that the "Lord is good" and "His mercy endures forever" (Ps. 100:5, 136:1).

+ Walk out on the battlefield *praising God* in advance for the victory!

Now it's your turn to pray:

Lord God of Jeshoshaphat, [compose your prayer as the Holy Spirit leads, drawing as needed from the bullet points above].

Chapter 7

THE PRAYER OF ELIJAH

*Lord God of Abraham, Isaac, and Israel, let it be known this
day that You are God in Israel and I am Your servant...*

1 Kings 18:36

Elijah the Tishbite was inarguably one of the most passionate, unforgettable, and influential of all the Old Testament prophets. He prophesied during the reigns of Ahab and Ahaziah in Northern Israel during the ninth century BC. His name means "my God is Yahweh," which itself was a proclamation of his main mission: to turn the children of Abraham back to the God of their forefathers. His life was undergirded by divine protection and provision, to the point that he was supernaturally fed three times: by ravens (1 Kings 17:1–6), by a widow (1 Kings 17:7–24), and by an angel (1 Kings 19:3–8). Eight miracles are attributed to Elijah in Scripture, the most remarkable being his deathless exit from this world in a whirlwind and a chariot of fire (2 Kings 2:11).

The pivotal event of his life was the confrontation with the prophets of Baal. It came at a time of great spiritual apostasy and a climate of extreme political corruption in Israel. The kingdom had fallen into the hands of Ahab and Jezebel. Ahab is identified as the wickedest king ever to rule over the seed of Abraham. He "did more to provoke the Lord God of Israel to anger than all the kings of Israel who were before him" (1 Kings 16:33).

Ahab's Gentile wife, Jezebel, a Phoenician princess, was, in barefaced language, a "royal witch." She was a crafty and cruel instigator of false religion who led an "entourage" of four hundred fifty Baal worshippers and four hundred prophets of Asherah (1 Kings 18:19). She despised anyone who attempted to restrain her unbridled lust for unlimited power and spiritual dominance. She was a master manipulator who used shameless sensuality to control a somewhat spineless husband and other weak males. So marked was this dark trait in Jezebel that her very name has since become a catchphrase for a woman who shows these kinds of evil tendencies.

Elijah's dramatic confrontation with the prophets of Baal, the god Jezebel worshipped, is recorded in the following passage:

> Then Elijah said to all the people, "Come near to me." So all the people came near to him. And he repaired the altar of the LORD that was broken down. And Elijah took twelve stones, according to the number of the tribes of the sons of Jacob, to whom the word of the LORD had come, saying, "Israel shall be your name." Then with the stones he built an altar in the name of the LORD; and he made a trench around the altar large enough to hold two seahs of seed. And he put the wood in order, cut the bull in pieces, and laid it on the wood, and said, "Fill four waterpots with water, and pour it on the burnt sacrifice and on the wood."
>
> And it came to pass, at the time of the offering of the evening sacrifice, that Elijah the prophet came near and said: *"LORD God of Abraham, Isaac, and Israel, let it be known this day that You are God in Israel and I am Your*

servant, and that I have done all these things at Your word. Hear me, O Lord, hear me, that this people may know that You are the Lord God, and that You have turned their hearts back to You again."

...Then the fire of the Lord fell and consumed the burnt sacrifice, and the wood and the stones and the dust, and it licked up the water that was in the trench. Now when all the people saw it, they fell on their faces; and they said, "The Lord, He is God! The Lord, He is God!"

—1 Kings 18:30–33, 36–39, emphasis added

God's Supernatural Response

Most likely Baal's prophets passed from brazen rebellion against God to an almost paralyzing, mind-gripping fear of Him in a split second. When Elijah prayed, it brought one of the most awe-inspiring responses from heaven ever to take place in the history of God's dealings with men. Fire fell from heaven and consumed the sacrifices on the altar Elijah built. The people immediately began shouting, "The Lord, He is God!" (or in Hebrew, *Yahweh, He is Elohim!*). The destruction of false religion in Israel happened in one day. A religious stronghold that had persisted for many decades came crashing down. Then Elijah prayed again and the drought ended. An abundance of rain was poured out on the land. Now let's examine point by point how this prayer of Elijah provoked God to dramatically demonstrate His power and apply it to our own prayer life.

Six "Power Points" in Elijah's Prayer

Let's look carefully at six "power points" revealed in Elijah's prayer.

Power point #1

> LORD God...
>
> —I KINGS 18:36

Notice that Elijah referred to the Most High as "LORD God" (actually, he would have spoken the name for God revealed to Moses, most likely *Yahweh Elohim*). This was a very important distinction for Elijah to make because eight hundred fifty false prophets were crying out to their deity using the name Baal as they cut themselves and danced into a religious frenzy. It was essential for the prophet Elijah, on that intense day of supernatural confrontation, to counter the false deity by addressing the only true God by His personal name.

The Hebrew word *Elohim*, which is translated "God," is more of a general term for the maker of heaven and earth, a word that even the Baal worshippers might have used concerning their deity. However, it hides a mystery. For even though *Elohim* is a plural word, it is translated into the singular word "God" over two thousand times in Scripture. So *Elohim* is a revelation of the plurality of the Godhead (Father, Son, and Holy Spirit—yet these three are one God).

God's personal name is probably either Yahweh or Yehovah. Drawn from the Hebrew letters YHWH, and traditionally called the Tetragrammaton, it was originally written in the Hebrew language with only consonants, no vowels. In most English Bibles YHWH is rendered "Lord" (thousands of times). But the word *Lord* simply means

"Master," so it is really an insufficient rendering. That would be like calling some man "Mister" instead addressing him by his personal name.

Unfortunately at some point in the history of Israel—because of numerous times of destruction, dispersion, and enslavement, and because of an excessive concern about breaking the third commandment—the correct pronunciation of YHWH was lost. Some contend that it should be pronounced "Jehovah," but that was never a revealed name; rather, it was a name merely "created" by a translator. Because there is no "J" sound in the Hebrew language some contend that it should be pronounced "Ye-ho-vah."

The contracted form of God's name is "YAH" (like the last syllable of the worship word "Hallelujah," which means "praise to YAH," or the Scripture, "Trust in the Lord forever, for in YAH, the Lord, is everlasting strength"—Isaiah 26:4). The loss of certainty in this weighty matter is a major calamity because worshippers who use God's personal name are affirming they have a personal relationship with the One who bears the name. This should automatically result in an outpouring of wisdom, revelation, favor, and power, just as it did for Elijah. We cannot go back and fix this dilemma stemming from the old covenant, but we now have a new covenant solution.

We can say with absolute assurance that the personal name of the Son of God is Jesus (or more perfectly in the Hebrew, *Yeshua*). Christians should go beyond merely referring to Him as the "Christ" or the "Messiah," which are just titles, both of which mean "the Anointed One." For instance, you should not say, "*Christ* saved me." Instead use His personal name, Jesus or Yeshua.

The Yahweh of the Old Testament is the Yeshua of the New Testament—because He always has been and always will be "the image of the invisible God" (Col. 1:15). Yeshua, which means "the salvation of God," is described as the "name which is above every name" (Phil. 2:9). Calling God by His personal name indicates you have rights to access the Father and all the divinely conferred privileges of salvation, including the amazing promise that He gave when He walked on the earth, "If you ask anything *in My name*, I will do it" (John 14:14, emphasis added).

Action step: *Declare to God that you know there is only one God and that He is triune in nature, and call the Lord by His name.*

Power point #2

> LORD God of Abraham, Isaac, and Israel...
>
> —1 KINGS 18:36

Elijah then added the names of the patriarchs to the name of the Lord, calling Him the "God of Abraham, Isaac, and Israel." By doing so he was making a powerful and multifaceted declaration. First, he was reminding God, "We have history! Because our forefathers were in a covenant relationship with You, we can expect a continuation of the promises and commitments You made to them."

At the burning bush God revealed Himself to Moses as "the God of Abraham, the God of Isaac, and the God of Jacob" and declared, "This is My name forever, and this is My memorial to all generations" (Exod. 3:15). This declaration should stir the coals of a burning question in our hearts: *Why would the perfect and flawless God of heaven name Himself with the names of imperfect and flawed men?*

It is because by doing so, God shows that He is not just an austere and distant Creator who is relatively uninvolved in the lives of His people. Instead He holds a very personal love toward any individual with whom He has a genuine relationship. He is not just the God of the universe in its immensity; He is the God who embraces us in our smallness. He is not just the God of a nation of nameless faces; He is the God of every individual in that covenant nation. Each person is supremely and infinitely important to Him.

The use of this name was also a prophetic way of declaring that what He did in the lives of the patriarchs, He can and will *do again*! Consider the following: calling Him the "God of Abraham" was a declaration that He is a God who will perform in our lives things similar to what He did in Abraham's life.

For instance, He is:

- ✦ A God who often calls those who are unqualified for their God-given task: Abraham and Sarah were both old and Sarah, apparently infertile, yet they were chosen to produce a multitude of offspring, like the "stars of the heaven" (Gen. 22:17).

- ✦ A God who raises dead things back to life: He quickened Abraham's "dead" body and Sarah's "dead" womb to bring forth Isaac (Rom. 4:19).

- ✦ A God who turns cursed people into a blessing: According to tradition, Abraham's father was a maker of idols. According to Deuteronomy 5:7–9 this results in a curse from God that is passed down to future generations. But God gave Abraham a chance to "break" the family curse by instead making him "a blessing" to future generations (Gen. 12:2).

Calling Him the "God of Isaac" was a declaration that He is:

+ A God who turns mourning into laughter: the name *Isaac* means "laughter," and was given to Abraham and Sarah's son because he created such laughter in the hearts of those who had mourned because of childlessness for so long.

+ A God who often fulfills promises after a long waiting period: it was twenty-five years before the promised son Isaac was born.

+ A God who causes a spiritual legacy and blessing to pass from one generation to the next.

Calling Him the "God of Israel" was a declaration that He is:

+ A God who often exalts those who seem least likely to succeed: Esau was literally the firstborn son, but Jacob was exalted to receive the double-portion, firstborn son status.

+ A God who wrestles with His people to subdue their carnal nature: the Angel of the Lord wrestled with Jacob all night long (Gen. 32:22–32).

+ A God who changes names and changes character: at the end of their "wrestling match" God changed the name *Jacob*, which possibly means "heel-catcher" or "supplanter" (one who takes that which is not his own) to the name "Israel," which

possibly means "prince of God," "the prince who
prevails with God" or "one who rules with God."

So by calling Him the "God of Abraham, Isaac, and
Israel," Elijah was declaring that God could do very similar
things again. He could raise Israel, a spiritually dead nation,
back to life. He could turn the curse (indicated by a lengthy
drought) into a blessing (indicated by an outpouring of rain).
He could turn their mourning into laughter and change the
backslidden seed of Jacob into true Israelites (those who rule
and reign with God)—all of which actually happened.

Action step: *Declare that your God is the God of Abraham, Isaac, and
Israel, and rehearse some of the significant, supernatural things
Yahweh did in their lives, expecting similar things to be repeated
for you.*

Power point #3

Let it be known this day that You are God in Israel…
—1 Kings 18:36

This is an appeal to Yahweh to display His sovereignty, to
express His authority, and to evidence His involvement in
the affairs of the seed of Abraham, thus revealing His covenant commitment to them.

Action step: *Ask God to supply proof of His reality through your life,
so unbelievers especially will know He is God!*

Power point #4

Lord God of Abraham, Isaac, and Israel, let it be known
this day that…I am your servant…
—1 Kings 18:36

When we sincerely acknowledge the Most High as our master, and ourselves as His servants, we are making a statement. We are declaring that we exist to fulfill His will alone, that we live and breathe to accomplish His purpose. Awesome promises are made in the Bible to those who can truly label themselves the servants of God, such as the following:

> "No weapon formed against you shall prosper, and every tongue which rises against you in judgment you shall condemn. This is the heritage of the servants of the Lord, and their righteousness is from Me," says the Lord.
>
> —ISAIAH 54:17

> And on my servants and on my handmaidens I will pour out in those days of my Spirit; and they shall prophesy.
>
> —ACTS 2:18

> His lord said to him, "Well done, good and faithful servant! You have been faithful over a few things, I will make you ruler over many things. Enter into the joy of your lord."
>
> —MATTHEW 25:23

Action step: *Declare that you exist to serve God and His purposes. Ask Him to respond with a supernatural witness of His approval.*

Power point #5

> LORD God of Abraham, Isaac, and Israel, let it be known this day that…I have done all these things at Your word.
>
> —1 KINGS 18:36

When the written Word is referred to in Scripture, the Greek term used is *logos*. When God is speaking in the present, the Greek term used is *rhema*. Jesus said, "The words that I speak to you are spirit, and they are life" (John 6:63).

The word translated "words" is *rhema*; the word translated "life" is *zoe* (pronounce zo-ay') which means "divine life." That is a great example of "the living Word" (something God is speaking in the present). His Word is full of the life of God.

There is great power in knowing just the *logos*. God's Word is forever settled in the heavens. Even Jesus battled Satan by declaring the *logos*. He countered each of Satan's three temptations by saying, "It is written." There are 7,487 promises in the *logos*. Those promises are obtained by faith (Heb. 11:33). Many miracles happen just by trusting in the written Word. Yet, there is an even greater power available to those who speak as the "oracles of God"—who become a conduit of what God is speaking in the present (1 Pet. 4:11).

Action step: *Remind God your petition is based on His infallible Word: the written Word or the living word.*

Power point #6

> Hear me, O LORD, hear me, that this people may know that You are the LORD God, and that You have turned their hearts back to You again.
>
> —1 KINGS 18:37

In other words, Elijah was saying to God, "It's not about me; it's about You and it's about them. The miracle of sending fire is for Your name's sake and for their benefit, to deliver them from false religion." Making this confession was also an admission that only God can change a heart. Elijah knew that he was powerless to transform people internally on his own.

Action step: *Emphasize that intervening in your situation is a means for God to show He is God and a means of turning hearts back to Him.*

My Experience With the Elijah Method of Praying

Back in the mideighties I conducted an open-air crusade in a densely populated city in South India called Kumbakonam. That area was a strong hub of the Hindu religion, filled with many temples and shrines. About four thousand people were in attendance, sitting on the ground and on surrounding walls and roofs.

The pastoral council told me that I was the first Western missionary to conduct a major campaign within the city limits and that such an accomplishment was extraordinary. Though most Hindu people are extremely gentle and tolerant, unknown to me, a group of radical Hindus had planned to storm the platform on the opening night of the crusade. They intended to beat me up publicly, tie me to the bumper of their car, and then drag me through the city, hoping they would shut down missionary activity in that region. God anticipated their plan, though, and prepared a miracle of divine intervention in advance.

As I closed my message that first night, I felt intense spiritual resistance. It was as if dozens of demons were closing in on me and gripping me around my throat. I had to force out every word as I "pushed" against evil principalities that had established spiritual strongholds in that region and had been relatively unopposed for centuries.

My mind almost succumbed to the pressure and accepted the idea that there would be hardly any results that night. Then right at the critical moment, God dropped a word of knowledge into my spirit: "Call for the deaf, and tell them that if what you have preached is true, every one of them will hear again—and if what you preached is not true, they won't hear and the people can throw you out of their city."

I trembled at the thought of using such a bold, "Elijah-like" tactic, but I had a *rhema* word from God. I knew it would work, and I had to obey. Little did I know how important obedience to God would be to me personally that night.

After I shouted out the challenge to the audience, one by one, seven deaf persons were escorted to the platform. Four were totally deaf, and three were deaf in only one ear. My faith was high, so I blurted out, "Bring me somebody first who is totally deaf" (little did I know how important that decision would prove to be). A young man about twenty-three years old was brought to me who had lost his hearing five years prior. I began to pray, commanding his ears to be opened in the name of the Lord.

Then suddenly, I heard a loud, slamming, bashing sound echoing through the whole platform area again and again. Everyone on the platform kept turning and looking in the direction of the sound. A twenty-foot-high, padlocked gate stood at the rear of the platform. It was supposed to prevent break-ins. No one knew that six radical Hindus had crept up the stairwell in the dark and were hitting the big padlock with a sledge hammer in order to knock it off.

Crash! The big lock finally gave way and hit the concrete, right when I was in the middle of praying for the young man to regain his hearing. I anxiously turned my head to look in the direction of the gate, concerned that something would steal the crowd's attention from the promised miracle. As the gate swung open, six men came running toward me, all of their faces darkened and twisted with an angry scowl. Then all at once the young man jerked out of my hands and began leaping for joy, shouting to the audience that he could hear again. The crowd erupted in excitement—and simultaneously the leader of the Hindu radical group abruptly stopped in his tracks, gazing at the young man dumbfounded. I had no idea what was going on.

That man, who had originally come to shut the meeting down, stepped forward and whispered into one of the ears of the young man, who promptly repeated his words. He whispered in his other ear, and the response was the same. Shaking his head in amazement, he called his cohorts over and they too began to test the miracle, making comments to one another such as, "God has truly worked a miracle!"

I know it sounds outrageous, but I then jumped to the conclusion that these men were a committee appointed by the supporting pastors to verify the miracles. While faith was high, I moved quickly, praying for the second person, who was healed, then the third person, who also was healed—until all seven received their hearing again. Incidentally all seven were checked and verified by the six men who actually came to beat me up (something I was oblivious to at the time).

Because God responded to the challenge, I gave an altar call and about five hundred Hindus came forward to give their lives to Jesus (including the six men who came to disrupt the service that night). I did not learn their true intent until we talked the next day. It was during our time of sharing that I discovered the real reason the leader had stopped so abruptly on the platform the night prior—*the first deaf person healed was his next-door neighbor.* So he knew without a doubt that the miracle was genuine. What a divinely orchestrated happening!

What About You?

Now it is time for you to pray, confess, and believe the power points in the Elijah prayer. The following bulleted statements summarize what we have learned in this chapter. After rehearsing these points, create your own prayer. Use as many parts of the Elijah prayer as you can. If at all possible, be sure to cover at least the six primary points:

+ Call upon the name of the Lord. Use as many of His redemptive names as possible.

+ Declare that He is the God of Abraham, Isaac, and Israel, rehearsing some of the significant, supernatural things Yahweh did in their lives.

+ Ask God to supply proof of His reality through your life so that unbelievers especially will know *He is God!*

+ Declare your commitment to servanthood—that you exist to serve God and His purposes.

+ Remind God that your petition is based on His infallible, unchanging, and undefeatable Word.

+ Finally, emphasize that intervention in your situation is primarily a means for God to show that He really is God and a means of turning the hearts of people back to Him.

Now it's time to pray:

Lord God of Elijah, [compose your prayer as the Holy Spirit leads, drawing as needed from the previous bullet points].

Chapter 8

THE PRAYER OF JONAH

But I will sacrifice to You with the voice of thanksgiving;
I will pay what I have vowed. Salvation is of the LORD.

JONAH 2:9

JONAH WAS THE first Hebrew prophet called of God to preach the word of the Lord to Gentiles. He was sent to the city of Nineveh, the capital of the Assyrian empire, which was an arch-enemy of Israel. He functioned in this prophetic calling around 820 BC, during the reign of Jeroboam II.[1] Apparently he had already prophesied to Israel at an earlier time (see 2 Kings 14:25).

Jonah's story is fairly well known. After resisting the call to preach to Nineveh, Jonah found himself on a sinking ship, then cast overboard, then in the belly of a great fish. Jonah's prayer while in the belly of that creature is our focus in this chapter:

> Then Jonah prayed to the LORD his God from the fish's belly. And he said: *"I cried out to the LORD because of my affliction, and He answered me. Out of the belly of Sheol I cried, and You heard my voice. For You cast me into the deep, into the heart of the seas, and the floods surrounded me; all Your billows and Your waves passed over me. Then I said, 'I have been cast out of Your sight; yet I will look again toward Your holy temple.' The waters surrounded me, even to my soul; the deep closed around me; weeds were wrapped around my head. I*

went down to the moorings of the mountains; the earth with its bars closed behind me forever; yet You have brought up my life from the pit, O Lord, my God. When my soul fainted within me, I remembered the Lord; and my prayer went up to You, into Your holy temple. Those who regard worthless idols [translated "lying vanities" in the kjv] forsake their own mercy. But I will sacrifice to You with the voice of thanksgiving; I will pay what I have vowed. Salvation is of the Lord."

—Jonah 2:1–9, emphasis added

As you can see, Jonah's prayer was not a cry for deliverance—it was essentially an outburst of praise. He was thanking God for answering a previous prayer and for rescuing him from the clutches of death. He was worshipfully reminding God that He had intervened for him in an impossible situation. Jonah celebrated that divine intervention by saying, "I cried out to the Lord because of my affliction, and He answered me. Out of the belly of Sheol [translated "out of the belly of hell" in the kjv] I cried, and You heard my voice" (Jon. 2:2).

Jonah suffered the consequences of his rebellion. Though called to prophesy to the people of Nineveh, he fled from the presence of the Lord and caught a ship to Tarshish. A terrible storm lashed out at the vulnerable sea vessel. Having exhausted all options, the men of the ship, hoping to calm the boisterous wind and waves, reluctantly tossed Jonah overboard. When the storm suddenly subsided, they were shocked into tossing away their idols and worshipping the true God (even in his rebellion God used the backslidden prophet to accomplish His purposes).

Obviously Jonah went under and Scripture suggests that he drowned before being swallowed by the fish. The Amplified Bible provides a more vivid description of what transpired: "The waters compassed me about, even to [the extinction of] life; the abyss surrounded me, the seaweed was wrapped about my head. Yet You have brought up my life from the pit and corruption, O Lord my God" (vv. 5–6).

Jonah not only recounted his physical body sinking to the bottom of the ocean, he also described a permanent spiritual incarceration: "I went down to the moorings of the mountains; the earth with its bars closed behind me forever" (v. 6).

The earth with its bars? Surely this was a reference to the dark prison of the underworld. Jesus revealed in His parable of the rich man and Lazarus that in that Old Testament era, the realm of the dead was divided into two chambers. The entire lower world is referred to as *Sheol* in the Hebrew language and *Hades* in the Greek. One chamber was for the wicked and the other for the righteous, with an impassable gulf between the two. (See Luke 16:19–31.)

As Jonah was guilty of blatant rebellion against the Most High, we can presume his soul sunk down to the dark, dreadful abode of the unrighteous. There in "the lower parts of the earth" (Eph. 4:9), he cried out in desperation.

Though normally no second chance is offered to those who go through the portal of death unprepared, there have been many documented cases in which God provided an "exception to the rule" (I personally know of two). Jonah had a lot to be thankful for, because it seems he was one of those exceptions.[2]

God's Supernatural Response

How did God respond to Jonah's prayer? First, He completed Jonah's deliverance. He had already delivered the prophet from the "belly of hell"; next, the Lord delivered him from the belly of the fish. God never does a partial work. What He starts, He finishes. "Whatever God does, it shall be forever. Nothing can be added to it, and nothing taken from it" (Eccles. 3:14).

Jonah's story also illustrates that at times God may *speak directly* to situations in our lives, commanding them to conform to His will. Jonah 2:10 reveals, "*The LORD spoke to the fish*, and it vomited Jonah onto dry land" (emphasis added).

God's second supernatural response was to bring a powerful spiritual awakening to the entire city of Nineveh, delivering the inhabitants from impending doom. After hearing Jonah's prophetic word, the entire populace of this large and wicked port city repented before the Lord. Here is the biblical account:

> Then word came to the king of Nineveh; and he arose from his throne and laid aside his robe, covered himself with sackcloth and sat in ashes. And he caused it to be proclaimed and published throughout Nineveh by the decree of the king and his nobles, saying,
>
> Let neither man nor beast, herd nor flock, taste anything; do not let them eat, or drink water. But let man and beast be covered with sackcloth, and cry mightily to God; yes, let every one turn from his evil way and from the violence that is in his hands. Who can tell if God will turn and relent, and turn away from His fierce anger, so that we may not perish?
>
> Then God saw their works, that they turned from their evil way; and God relented from the disaster that He had said He would bring upon them, and He did not do it.
>
> —JONAH 3:6-10

What an amazing miracle of divine intervention! In the history of God's dealings with men there has never been such a complete, citywide spiritual awakening. (Oh, God, do it again!)

Some claim that Jonah's story is just a biblical myth, a spiritual allegory that teaches us valuable lessons. However, Jesus referred to Jonah's miraculous deliverance as a fact, not mere legend. Read His assessment:

> He answered and said to them, "An evil and adulterous generation seeks after a sign, and no sign will be given to it except *the sign of the prophet Jonah*. For as Jonah was three days and three nights in the belly of the great fish, so will the Son of Man be three days and three nights in the heart of the earth. The men of Nineveh will rise up in the judgment with this generation and condemn it, because they repented at the preaching of Jonah; and indeed a greater than Jonah is here."
>
> —MATTHEW 12:39–41, EMPHASIS ADDED

Yes, because "a greater than Jonah" has now come, we can expect greater acts of supernatural power. When we pray, we must boldly believe that God is still *God* and that miracles on this grand scale can still come to pass.

Seven "Power Points" in Jonah's Prayer

Let's look now at seven important "power points" revealed in the prayer of Jonah.

Power point #1

> I cried out to the LORD because of my affliction, and He answered me.
>
> —JONAH 2:2

Afflictions in life (mental, emotional, or physical) should push us to pray. They should motivate us to seek God and believe for a miracle. Sometimes the opposite happens. Overwhelmed by sorrow, pain, disappointment, or rejection, people sometimes become hardened in sorrow. (See Job 6:10.) They give up. They pull away from their Redeemer-God, their primary source of help, thinking that there is no hope. May it instead be said of us, "We are not of those who draw back to perdition, but of those who believe to the saving of the soul" (Heb. 10:39).

Jonah refused to give up, even when hope seemed lost. The Scripture gives new covenant people an even greater hope. Speaking of the Messiah and His people, Scripture says, "In all their afflictions, He was afflicted" (Isa. 63:9; see also Ps. 22:24). In other words, on the cross He felt our afflictions as if they were His own. You can expect divine intervention from Him. He knows what you are going through. It may not be *what* you want, *when* you want, *the way* you want— but one way or the other, God will answer.

Action step: *Determine that afflictions will only push you toward God and that God feels your pain.*

Power point #2

> I have been cast out of Your sight; yet I will look again toward Your holy temple.
>
> —Jonah 2:4

The name *Jonah* means "dove." I can't help but think those Jewish parents missed it when naming their son. Either they were not inspired, or maybe they listened to the wrong advice. They should have called their baby boy *Chamor* (Hebrew for "donkey"). This man was no gentle, submissive bird. Let's be real: he had the nature of a donkey, usually pulling directly opposite to God's will. In fact, you could probably put Jonah's picture next to the word *obstinate* in the dictionary.

First, he obstinately refused to preach to the Ninevites, even though it was *the almighty God* who told him to do it. (Yikes! What kind of fool would do that?) Then, having drowned, he stubbornly refused to just sink into the darkness and accept the eternal judgment he deserved. (How headstrong can you get?) Instead, he asserted, "I will look again toward Your holy temple." For Jonah, looking toward the temple meant looking toward the holy of holies, where the ark of the covenant resided. The ark was a sacred object upon which sat the mercy seat, which was God's representative throne on earth. So in essence Jonah was saying, "I am believing that mercy will prevail for me. Have mercy upon me, O Father of mercies, and give me another chance."

God likes that kind of fighting-faith attitude. What if Jonah had just submitted to his fate? What if he had said, "I am cut off from God. There is no hope for me." The story would have ended quite differently. The Ninevites never would have repented. Their city would have been destroyed. And the erring prophet would have been listed with other infamous biblical characters such as Dathan, Korah, Abiram, Balaam, and Judas. Instead, he is honored in the biblical Hall of Fame. Being raised out of the grips of corruption, he became a symbol of the Messiah yet to come. (See Matthew 12:29–31, 16:4; Luke 11:29–32.)

So stubbornness can be a good thing—if it's sanctified and channeled in the right direction. No matter how terribly you've failed, even if it seems that God has cast you out of His sight—hold on and believe. When all hope seems to be gone, dare to gaze heavenward and cry, "O Father, I will look toward Your holy temple—the true temple and the true throne—in the heaven of heavens. I admit that I have not walked in perfect obedience to all You have commanded, but I believe Your mercy will restore my soul, my gifts, my vision, and my purpose."

If it worked for Jonah before the cross, when the blood of a mere goat was sprinkled on the mercy seat on Yom Kippur (the Day of Atonement), how much more should stubborn faith work for us now that the blood of the Son of God has been shed for us?

Action step: *Tell God you intend to hold on to Him and to ever gaze toward His heavenly throne.*

Power point #3

> When my soul fainted within me, I remembered the LORD.
> —JONAH 2:7

When you're in a crisis, when you're fainting spiritually— shutting down mentally and emotionally from the pressure you are facing—what should you do? Exactly what Jonah did—remember! Remember who God is, what He has promised, and how He has proven Himself in the past:

+ Remember God's declaration, "I have loved you with an everlasting love" (Jer. 31:3).
+ Remember God's promise, "I will never leave you nor forsake you" (Heb. 13:5).

+ Remember God's assurance, "The gifts and the calling of God are irrevocable" (Rom. 11:29).

+ Remember God's revelation, "You did not choose Me, but I chose you" (John 15:16).

+ Remember God's commitment to be the "author and finisher" of your faith (Heb. 12:2).

+ Remember that He who began a good work in you "will complete it until the day of Jesus Christ" (Phil. 1:6).

Furthermore, remember all the good things God has uniquely and personally done for you—every deliverance, every healing, and every miracle of divine intervention. Then dare to declare that what God has done in the past He will yet do in the future—simply because Jesus is "the same yesterday, today, and forever" (Heb. 13:8).

Action step: *Remember and rehearse some of God's promises and what He has done for you in the past.*

Power point #4

Those who regard worthless idols forsake their own mercy.
—JONAH 2:8

"Worthless idols" is a reference to carved or engraved images of false deities. Or a "worthless idol" can be any person, goal, possession, desire, or thing human beings dare to place above God. Even "covetousness" (an inordinate desire for unnecessary material things) is referred to as "idolatry" (Col. 3:5).

The King James Version translates the phrase "worthless idols" as "lying vanities." So it could also mean any delusional, false, carnal belief. Jonah did not worship a false god, but he did harbor the vain delusion that he could get away with ignoring the true God's command, so his decision was a "lying vanity."

It could have been the result of pride ("I am a Jew. I don't mingle with Gentiles."), prejudice ("The Ninevites are wicked. They're corrupt. They are not in covenant with God."), or fear ("They might kill me!"). Any one of these motives could have become idolatrous and worthless if it dethroned God and His will. But having sunk into *Sheol*, Jonah painfully admitted, "My attitude was an idol! I exalted my opinion above God's opinion. In doing so, I removed God from His throne. Now I make a commitment to tear down my idols to show God how serious I am about serving Him!"

Action step: *Renounce all "worthless idols" and "lying vanities."*

Power point #5:

> I will sacrifice to You with the voice of thanksgiving.
> —JONAH 2:9

Jonah knew at this major crisis point that no animal sacrifice could be offered to provide a suitable atonement. It was too late, and his sin was too great. Instead, Jonah decided to offer a sacrifice of thanksgiving for what God had already done in his life. Remember, he wasn't wholly delivered yet. He had been released from hell but not from the belly of the great fish. Apparently he was conscious inside of the creature. Even though his deliverance wasn't yet complete, he determined to express gratitude over the partial miracle already accomplished. That should speak to every one of us. We may not have received total deliverance in certain areas just yet, but let's be thankful for what God has done.

At one point in the English language, the word *thank* was the past tense of the word *think* (like the words *drank* and *drink*, or *stank* and *stink*).[3] Though the two words have taken altogether different roads of meaning, in reality they are still very related, because if we don't "think," we won't "thank"—if we don't "think" about how good God has been to us, we will rarely "thank" Him for His many blessings.

Gratitude is one of the most important attitudes for a prayerful person to manifest when approaching God's throne. We are commanded to "enter His gates with thanksgiving" (Ps. 100:4) and "in everything by prayer and supplication, with thanksgiving," let our requests be made known to God (Phil. 4:6).

God really responds to a thankful heart. Remember how Jesus praised the one out of ten cleansed lepers who rushed back to give thanks to God. The Messiah announced that his faith had made him "whole" (Luke 17:19, KJV). Leprosy often results in open, running sores and, frequently, missing fingers and toes (something very distressing to see; I have preached in a leper colony in India). I tend to believe that the thankful leper received not just cleansing (sealing up the festered sores) but also wholeness (complete restoration of the missing parts of his body). Certainly God has not changed. He still rewards thankful hearts, not only with healing but also with wholeness.

Thankfulness over *past* blessings and benefits is a potent way of counteracting fear, depression, discouragement, and a host of other negatives that plague us in the *present*. It focuses our minds on the good instead of the evil, on what's right instead of what's wrong. It is very attractive to God and should be attractive to us.

Thankfulness over expectations for the *future* is one of the highest forms of faith. To thank God in advance for His keeping power, for deliverance from every trial, for divine health, for prosperity, or for any other thing is a way of saying, "It is as good as done." We don't know if Jonah made a commitment to thank God for past benefits or future expectations, but we do know his gratitude was a pivot on which a tremendous miracle turned. And if he could do it when he was *literally* swallowed up by negative circumstances, certainly we can as well.

Action step: *Enter God's gates with thanksgiving!*

Power point #6

> I will pay what I have vowed.
>
> —JONAH 2:9

To vow is to make a commitment before God to do a certain thing or give a certain amount. Vows are sacred. They are taken very seriously in heaven. When a person makes a vow but fails to follow through, Ecclesiastes 5:1 labels it "the sacrifice of fools." The Scripture warns:

> When you vow a vow to God, do not wait to pay it. For He has no pleasure in fools. Pay that which you have vowed. It is better that you should not vow, than that you should vow and not pay.
>
> —ECCLESIASTES 5:4-5, MKJV

We don't know what promises Jonah had made to God that were broken or ignored. Neither do we know what commitments he had made to fellow human beings in the name of God that had been forgotten or neglected. But we do know that recommitting in this area brought God's renewed favor.

Lack of integrity with regard to vow-keeping is equal to a lie, and we know that God hates "a lying tongue" (Prov. 6:16–17). Therefore, renewed commitment to vows is attractive to the "God of truth" (Isa. 65:16) who promises to respond by pouring out on His submitted ones the "Spirit of truth" (John 15:26) and by activating the "word of truth" (2 Cor. 6:7) in their lives.

Action step: *Renew and fulfill vows you have made to God.*

Power point #7

> Salvation is of the LORD!
> —JONAH 2:9

The word *salvation* means "deliverance." It can mean deliverance from fear, enemies, sin, sickness, death, our fleshly bodies, even from eternal judgment. Those who confess that "salvation is of the Lord" are admitting that we human beings cannot save ourselves. The enemies of our souls are too strong, and within ourselves we are too weak. Therefore, we are completely dependent on God.

The name *Jesus* (*Yeshua*) appropriately means "the salvation of God" and the promise has been given, "Whoever calls on the name of the LORD shall be saved" (Acts 2:21). He is referred to in Scripture as:

+ **The tower of salvation**, into whom we run in times of trouble (2 Sam. 22:51)

- **The strength of our salvation,** who covers us in "the day of battle" (Ps. 140:7)

- **The rock of our salvation,** to whom we "shout joyfully" (Ps. 95:1)

- **The horn of our salvation,** who calls us to worship and warfare and brings the manifestation of the presence (2 Sam. 22:3)

- **The captain of our salvation,** who was made "perfect through suffering" (Heb. 2:10)

- **The God of our salvation,** who purges our sins for His name's sake (Ps. 79:9).

- **The author of eternal salvation** "to all who obey Him" (Heb. 5:9).

Our responsibility is to believe in who He is and to come into alignment with His Word and will. When we do, our Savior promises to save us from all our enemies. Who knows? Jonah may have been thinking of one of David's writings when he made this statement, such as Psalm 138:7–8:

> Though I walk in the midst of trouble, You will revive me; You will stretch out Your hand against the wrath of my enemies, *and Your right hand will save me.* The LORD will perfect that which concerns me; Your mercy, O LORD, endures forever; do not forsake the works of Your hands.
>
> —EMPHASIS ADDED

Action step: *Declare God to be your sole source of salvation.*

My Father's Remarkable Salvation

The following narrative emphasizes and magnifies a major aspect of the Jonah prayer—the amazing power of gratitude. This example is particularly close to my heart; it is the remarkable story of the salvation of my own father.

After being born again in the fall of 1970, I became very zealous about sharing this wonderful opportunity with all my relatives, especially my immediate family. Well, let me rephrase that, I wasn't just zealous, I was a little, shall I say, *overzealous and overbearing?* But having found the truth after searching so hard, I couldn't imagine being discreet about it.

Many of my family members responded with appreciation and readily received the Lord into their hearts. In fact, my mother was one of my first "converts" and was baptized in the Holy Spirit shortly afterward. But my father was somewhat taken aback by it all. He was a highly respected former military man (commander of three US naval destroyers). He was a good man—honest, moral, ethical—but set in his religious beliefs, which were distinctly different from my newfound fundamental, evangelical, Pentecostal/charismatic views drawn from Scripture.

My mother and I began seeking God diligently on his behalf and continued for over a decade. She went so far as to go on a forty-day fast, asking God to manifest Himself to my father supernaturally. One of our daily rituals was to claim Acts 16:31: "Believe on the Lord Jesus Christ, and thou shalt be saved, and thy house" (KJV).

Just when we were on the verge of losing hope that he would ever experience spiritual rebirth through the Lord Jesus, God came through in a very unexpected and unusual way. The master playwright set the stage for an unforgettable, dramatic entrance into my father's life. Overnight he developed a very serious neck condition. Apparently a disc had slipped out of place in his upper spinal column, and for seven days his head was locked in a bowed position. Everything he did—from eating to talking to reading the newspaper—he did with his head bent over. Finally, he couldn't endure it any longer. He checked in to the hospital late one afternoon, hoping some medical procedure would alleviate his pain.

Later on that night, alone in his hospital room with nothing else to do, he decided since he was already in the right position, he might as well pray. (When he told me about his decision, the thought went through my mind, *"Subtle hint from heaven, Dad!"*) Having retired from the Navy, my father had become a successful accountant, so he tended to be very precise in everything he did. He was very organized and prone to ordering things in a logical sequence. This trait filtered into his prayer time that night. He decided to go back to his earliest memories and review his entire life, thanking God for every good and beneficial thing that had ever come his way. That took him two hours.

He admitted, "I finally ran out of things to thank God for, so I decided just to praise Him because He is God." (I thought, *"Dad, you didn't know it, but you were exercising a biblical principle. Psalm 100:4 commands, 'Enter into His gates with thanksgiving and into His courts with praise.'"*) Then excitedly he blurted out, "You won't believe what happened to me then, Mike."

"Oh, yes, I will," I countered, "I've been praying for you for twelve years."

Then he began to relate to me one of the most amazing visions I have ever heard about. Knowing my father's deep commitment to honesty, I never doubted the authenticity of his experience. I knew if it weren't true, he wouldn't say it.

My excitement grew as he continued: "While I was praising God, a golden light came into the hospital room. Then the face of Jesus appeared in that light: battered, beaten, bleeding, and crowned with thorns. Then suddenly the golden light changed into a crimson red, and red light began pouring over me. I knew in my heart I was being washed in the blood of Jesus, and I knew I was being born again."

Shaking my head with astonishment I thought to myself, "He wasn't even asking to be saved—what an amazing visitation!"

For about a month my father was often overwhelmed with fresh gratitude. Every time he tried to describe what happened that night, he would just burst out weeping with a heart full of joy. He was a changed man from that day forward and ended up, years later, becoming an adult Sunday school teacher at a country church in Canton, North Carolina, where he and my mother retired.

I have always been awed by the fact that my father never actually asked for the experience he received, yet God gave him one of the most powerful salvation experiences of anyone I know. He simply made a sincere commitment to give thanks to God. So the spiritual law—"Give and it shall be given to you"—must work toward God as well as toward men. Thankfulness rescued Jonah and brought him out of an impossible situation, and thankfulness radically transformed my father. If it birthed such a spiritual breakthrough for them, then if our root motive is genuine, it might just work the same for you and me.

What About You?

Now it is time for you to pray, confess, and believe the power points in the Jonah prayer. The following bulleted statements summarize what we have learned in this chapter. After rehearsing these points, create your own prayer. Use as many parts of the Jonah prayer as you can, especially the seven points specified.

+ Begin, as Jonah did, by thanking God for having responded to your prayers in the past.

+ Determine that afflictions will only push you toward God.

+ Maintain stubborn faith, even if you feel like a failure.

+ Tell God you intend to tenaciously gaze toward His throne.

+ Remember the good things God has done for you in the past.

+ Renounce all "worthless idols" and "lying vanities."

+ Enter God's gates with thanksgiving.

+ Renew former commitments and vows to God.

+ Declare that the Most High is your sole source of salvation.

Now it's your turn to pray:

Lord God of Jonah, [compose your prayer as the Holy Spirit leads, drawing from the previous bullet points].

Chapter 9

THE PRAYER OF HEZEKIAH

O Lord of hosts, God of Israel, the One who dwells
between the cherubim, You are God, You alone, of all the
kingdoms of the earth. You have made heaven and earth.

Isaiah 37:16

Hezekiah was twenty-five years old when he became the twelfth king of Judah around 726 BC. His name means "the strength of Yahweh." Though the son of corrupt King Ahaz, he still emerged as one of eight good kings who reigned over Judah (a list that would include celebrated rulers such as Asa, Jehoshaphat, and Josiah).

Second Kings 18:5–7 gives the glowing portrayal:

> He trusted in the Lord God of Israel, so that after him was none like him among all the kings of Judah, nor who were before him. For he held fast to the Lord; he did not depart from following Him, but kept His commandments, which the Lord had commanded Moses. The Lord was with him; he prospered wherever he went.

Hezekiah's first act was to cleanse and repair the temple that had been neglected for many years. He renewed a covenant relationship with the God of Abraham, Isaac, and Jacob, and reinstated true worship, even celebrating Passover for an unprecedented two weeks.

He was a great champion against idolatry, even destroying the overly venerated "brazen serpent"—an object that had once been used to transmit healing to Israelites who were bitten by venomous serpents during their wilderness journey. As his soldiers broke it into pieces, Hezekiah named it Nehushtan, which means "a trifling thing of brass."[1] So evidently this righteous king was spiritual enough to recognize that it was not the brazen serpent that healed, but the God who used it as a point of contact. He saw beyond the practice of religious superstition to the supernatural reality of a true relationship with the almighty God.

To appreciate Hezekiah's prayer we must understand the context. In 721 BC the Assyrian army under Sennacherib invaded and destroyed the northern kingdom of Israel. Around that time the Jews of the southern kingdom began paying tribute to Sennacherib. But at a certain point Hezekiah refused to continue this practice, and Sennacherib marched on Jerusalem with a massive army. His representative, Rabshakeh, reviled them for their rebellion and ridiculed them for their faith in God with statements such as, "Beware lest Hezekiah persuade you, saying, 'The LORD will deliver us.' Has any one of the gods of the nations delivered its land from the hand of the king of Assyria?" (Isa. 36:18).

However, Hezekiah had received a prophecy from Isaiah three years prior that foretold the destruction of the Assyrian army:

> Therefore thus says the Lord GOD of hosts: "O My people, who dwell in Zion, do not be afraid of the Assyrian. He shall strike you with a rod....It shall come to pass in that day that his burden will be taken away from your

shoulder, and his yoke from your neck, and the yoke will be destroyed because of the anointing."

—Isaiah 10:24, 27

So when Hezekiah received a letter from Sennacherib filled with taunts, insults, and threats, he took it before the Lord:

And Hezekiah received the letter from the hand of the messengers, and read it; and Hezekiah went up to the house of the Lord, and spread it before the Lord.

Then Hezekiah prayed to the Lord, saying: "O Lord of hosts, God of Israel, the One who dwells between the cherubim, You are God, You alone, of all the kingdoms of the earth. You have made heaven and earth. Incline Your ear, O Lord, and hear; open Your eyes, O Lord, and see; and hear all the words of Sennacherib, which he has sent to reproach the living God. Truly, Lord, the kings of Assyria have laid waste all the nations and their lands, and have cast their gods into the fire; for they were not gods, but the work of men's hands—wood and stone. Therefore they destroyed them. Now therefore, O Lord our God, save us from his hand, that all the kingdoms of the earth may know that You are the Lord, You alone."

Then Isaiah the son of Amoz sent to Hezekiah, saying, "Thus says the Lord God of Israel, 'Because you have prayed to Me against Sennacherib king of Assyria, this is the word which the Lord has spoken concerning him: "The virgin, the daughter of Zion, has despised you, laughed you to scorn; the daughter of Jerusalem Has shaken her head behind your back!

"Whom have you reproached and blasphemed? Against whom have you raised your voice, and lifted up your eyes on high? Against the Holy One of Israel.""

—Isaiah 37:14–23

God's Supernatural Response

God responded supernaturally to Hezekiah's prayer by sending an angel of the Lord into the camp of the Assyrians. In one night's time one hundred eighty-five thousand of them were slaughtered by this invisible heavenly being. The few soldiers who remained went back to their homeland defeated. Miraculously the Israelites were spared without an arrow being shot or a spear being thrown. What was it about Hezekiah's prayer that provoked that kind of powerful response from God?

Three "Power-Points" in Hezekiah's Prayer

There are three important "power points" revealed in the prayer of Hezekiah that we must understand. Let's look at each carefully.

Power point #1

> O LORD of hosts, God of Israel, the One who dwells between the cherubim, You are God, You alone, of all the kingdoms of the earth. You have made heaven and earth.
>
> —ISAIAH 37:16

To describe God as "the One who dwells between the cherubim" was first a reference to the ark of the covenant that was behind the veil in the temple. Its lid, made of one piece of gold, had two cherubim of gold facing the glory of God that rested on the mercy seat. Also in the temple of Solomon, there were two larger cherubim standing on either side of the ark, facing outward, the wings of which touched each other and also touched the walls on either side. To reference the cherubim was a way of declaring that Israel was praying to:

+ The true God of heaven, whose presence was in their midst

+ The God of Moses, who had established a covenant with them at Mount Sinai where He gave the design of the ark

+ The God who had provided atonement for them (yearly, on Yom Kippur, the Day of Atonement, the blood of a goat was sprinkled on the mercy seat), making them a forgiven people, reconciled to God

However, the temple and its furniture were merely a "copy and shadow of the heavenly things" (Heb. 8:5). So with these words Hezekiah was declaring that a connection existed between the holy of holies in the temple and the true holy of holies in the uppermost celestial world. He and the rest of the children of Israel were declaring that they had supernatural "clout." The Israelites knew that, on the highest level, they were appealing in prayer to the God of all gods, who dwells between the living cherubim in the highest heavens, at the very apex of the spiritual universe.

The cherubim are unique celestial beings that have the faces of four creatures (a bullock, a lion, an eagle, and a man). They are full of eyes before and behind, within and without, and ceaselessly cry, "Holy, holy, holy, Lord God Almighty, who was, and is, and is to come" (Rev. 4:8, see also Ezek. 1:5–10). It was their charge in the beginning to "guard the way to the tree of life" (Gen. 3:24). So to appeal to the "One who dwells between the cherubim" is to say, "Almighty God, there is no god higher than You, and no authority greater than You. You are omnipotent, omnipresent, and omniscient. Like the cherubim full of eyes, in Your infinite knowledge You see all things in the past and in the future, all things internal and external, hidden and manifested. You intend to take us back to the dominion Adam lost in the beginning and to the tree of life, the source of everlasting life. All other gods are false. All other gods are powerless. You are holy and all the kingdoms of the world are subject to You."

Action step: *Acknowledge God as "the One who dwells between the cherubim," the One who has infinite knowledge and infinite existence. He is the maker of heaven and earth!*

Power point #2

> Incline Your ear, O Lord, and hear; open Your eyes, O Lord, and see; and hear all the words of Sennacherib, which he has sent to reproach the living God.
>
> —Isaiah 37:17

This is an appeal to God to intercept the diabolical plans of the enemy and an invitation to Him to own the battle. Hezekiah was sharing with God that if the Jews were brought to reproach, God Himself would be brought to reproach—for the enemy had declared that the God of the Jews was powerless to deliver them.

Action step: *Ask God to incline His ears and eyes to hear what satanic forces are plotting against you and overthrow their plans. Ask Him to own your battle by saying, "God, do not let the devils bring You to reproach!" It's God's battle, not yours!*

Power point #3

> Now therefore, O LORD our God, save us from his hand,
> that all the kingdoms of the earth may know that You are
> the LORD, You alone.
>
> —ISAIAH 37:20

The Hebrew word *yasha* is translated "save"; it is also rendered "defend," "deliver," "rescue," and "preserve." He is "God our Savior" (1 Tim. 2:3), "the Savior of the world" (John 4:42), and "the Savior of all men" (1 Tim. 4:10). The very name *Yeshua* (*Jesus*) means "the salvation of God," and His name is a declaration of His nature. This is who He is. This is what He does. He saves—and it's all for His glory!

Action step: *Ask God to save you—to defend, deliver, rescue, and preserve you. Declare His Savior titles over your life and ask Him to deliver you so that others will see His glory!*

My Encounter With an Angel

All through the Bible we find angels involved in protecting God's people and providing for them in times of need. They war against the enemy of our souls. Michael the archangel withstood Satan when he was minded toward abducting Moses's body. The angel simply said, "The Lord rebuke you!" and Satan was overcome (Jude 9). Satanic forces still seek to overpower believers, but surely, unknown to us, heavenly beings are still shouting, "The Lord rebuke you!" in our defense.

Each of us from birth has certain angels assigned to us who always behold the face of the Father in heaven (Matt. 18:10). According to this passage, angelic protectors are always watching over us. An equally powerful promise is given to those who dwell "in the secret place of the Most High" (Ps. 91:1): "For He shall give His angels charge over you, to keep you in all your ways" (v. 11).

Though I have often sensed the presence of angels in my evangelistic meetings, I have actually seen an angel only once. It was in a powerful prophetic dream that God gave me back in the mideighties. I saw a man of God holding a large scroll that was three or four feet wide. Then a radiant, tall angel came up and wrote on the scroll these words:

HEALING IS THE EXPRESSION OF GOD'S LOVE!

This statement may seem overly simplistic to some, but at the time it spoke very profoundly to me. Without realizing it, I had fallen into the error of thinking I almost had to "force God's hand" by quoting His Word until He felt obligated to fulfill it. Instead, God was letting me know that His fundamental motive for healing people is simply His love toward them and His desire to alleviate their suffering. The words kept rolling through my spirit, *"Healing is the expression of God's love. Healing is the expression of God's love."* Then from a distance (in the dream) I heard another man of God cry at the top of his voice:

"THERE ARE EVEN SOME WHO WILL RECEIVE CREATIVE POWER!"

At that point the dream came to an abrupt halt! I woke up with a jolt, with those words echoing inside of me. "Creative power," I thought. "That means parts of the body that are missing or dysfunctional will supernaturally be restored." Then God spoke to me to go on a lengthy fast. He promised that if I would obey, the depth of the anointing spoken of in the dream would be released in my ministry. Forty days later I announced a healing service because I had completed the fast and obeyed God's command.

That night a woman came to the service who was seriously handicapped. One leg was twisted from a car wreck and the other was twisted from a birth abnormality. During my message I shared the dream God had given me and the *rhema* (God-uttered as opposed to written) word He had spoken concerning the lengthy fast I was to complete. Then I gave an invitation for those who wanted a "creative miracle." The woman inched her way to the front, struggling the whole way, dragging her uncooperative legs, even throwing her body forward with her shoulders.

When she got right in front of me, I laid hands on her and prayed. As Hezekiah appealed to the God who dwells between the cherubim, I cried out to the God who sent His angel to me with that prophetic word. Immediately the woman was thrown to the floor by the power of God as His virtue coursed through her body. When she got up, she ran around the church building. I have never seen a miracle any more instantaneous and undeniable as that one. Was that same angel present? I don't know. But I do know that an angel brought the revelation in the beginning that healing is the expression of God's love, and my perspective and ministry were transformed.

If one angel can defeat an entire heathen army that had been the scourge of the earth in Hezekiah's day, one angel can bring miraculous intervention for us in our needs! Our God is the God who dwells between the cherubim, the God who surrounds us with "ministering spirits" who come to "minister for those who will inherit salvation" (Heb. 1:14). Notice that salvation and angels are connected in this passage out of Hebrews. I believe this indicates that one of the signs of our "salvation" is angelic intervention. Our Savior is the Lord of hosts, the God of an army of angels who are poised and ready for battle! If God can send an angel to defeat Israel's foes, expect Him to do it again for you!

What About You?

Now it is time for you to pray, confess, and believe the power points in the Hezekiah prayer. The following bulleted statements summarize what we have learned in this chapter. After rehearsing these points, create your own prayer. Use as many parts of the Hezekiah prayer as you can, especially the three points specified.

+ Declare that your God is the One who dwells between the cherubim.
+ Declare that all the kingdoms of the world are subject to His authority.
+ Declare that He is the Creator, the maker of heaven and earth.
+ Ask God to listen to, and see with His eyes, all the plots the enemy is waging against you.
+ Confess that any defeat coming to you would bring reproach to God.
+ Ask God to save you (defend, deliver, rescue, and preserve you) so that everyone who sees His blessing in your life will acknowledge Him as the source—that He and He alone will receive the glory!

+ Praise God using His Savior titles, especially the name of Jesus (Yeshua), which means "the salvation of God"!

+ Declare that your God is "the Lord of hosts" (the God of an army of angels) and ask Him to send angelic intervention in your life.

Now it's your turn to pray:

Lord God of Hezekiah, [compose your prayer drawing as needed from the bullet points above].

Chapter 10

THE PRAYER OF THE EARLY CHURCH

Now, Lord, look on their threats, and grant to Your servants
that with all boldness they may speak Your word, by stretching
out Your hand to heal, and that signs and wonders may
be done through the name of Your holy Servant Jesus.

ACTS 4:29–30

T HE WORD CHURCH comes from the Greek word *ekklesia,*
which simply means "the called out ones." Though
ekklesia (pronounced ek-klay-see'-ah) is usually translated
"church," it has been rendered "assembly" a few times. It can
be used to mean a local community of believers who assemble
together for worship and the study of God's Word, or it can
be global in scope, referring to all truly saved persons under
the new covenant. Those who qualify as the *ekklesia* do not
just go to church; they are the church.

So this common biblical term does not refer to a building
set aside for worship or to an organization. On the contrary,
the church is an organism—a living body of believers who
are united by a common experience of heart. There are many
different "churches" (denominational groups) with different
worship styles or doctrinal variations, but only one "true

church," which is made up of all born-again believers, regardless of their affiliation.

Unfortunately the word *church* has become an all-inclusive term for all who call themselves "Christian." However, just as "they are not all Israel who are of Israel" (Rom. 9:6), they are not all "the church" who claim to be in "the church."

Globally there are more than two billion people in what could be called *the professing church*—those who *profess* belief in the historical existence of the Lord Jesus Christ and who intellectually adhere to the value of what He accomplished through His death, burial, and resurrection (the salvation of the human race). However, there is a smaller core group within the professing church that could be termed the *possessing church*, those who actually *possess* a relationship with the Savior.

This element is essential because Jesus explained, "And this is eternal life, that they may know You, the only true God, and Jesus Christ whom You have sent" (John 17:3). It's not enough to just *know about* God (the professing church); it is essential to *know* God (the possessing church).

When the true church prays in faith, heaven responds—for of all people on the face of the earth, they have the connection necessary to bring divine intervention to bear on negative circumstances. They have the ear of God. They are "the pillar and foundation of the truth" (1 Tim. 3:15, MKJV) and God's conduit of power to bring about true revival.

Far too often those who belong to "the church" live beneath their privileges, failing to fully realize the influence they have in heaven. Far too often they do not bother praying and allow negative circumstances to rule unopposed.

As author F. B. Meyer so aptly stated, "The greatest tragedy of life is not unanswered prayer, but unoffered prayer."[1]

This chapter provides the prime New Testament example of how powerfully the throne room of God can be accessed in this present era by those who love the Lord Jesus Christ. How powerful it was then! How powerful it still is now!

To understand the prayer of the early church, one must know the climate in which it was prayed. As soon as the church was "born" on the Day of Pentecost, violent opposition rose up against it. Jesus had prophesied this kind of backlash when He said kingdom would rise up against kingdom. (See Matthew 24:7.) On the highest level He may have been referring to the kingdom of darkness and the kingdom of light, how they bash and slam into each other, resulting in outbreaks of revival and harsh, antagonistic reactions from those who are deceived and carnally minded. Like continental plates grating against each other, triggering earthquakes as they vie for the dominant position, so it is with the world and the church.

At the time this prayer of the early church was spoken, Peter and John had recently prayed for a lame man to walk, and the resulting miracle had created quite a stir. As a result, these two apostles were incarcerated overnight and told not to preach any more in the name of Jesus. The church's counterattack was to pray—to intercede and ask for divine intervention:

> So when they had further threatened them [Peter and John], they let them go, finding no way of punishing them, because of the people, since they all glorified God for what had been done. For the man was over forty years old on whom this miracle of healing had been performed.
>
> And being let go, they went to their own companions and reported all that the chief priests and elders had said

to them. So when they heard that, they raised their voice to God with one accord and said: "Lord, You are God, who made heaven and earth and the sea, and all that is in them, who by the mouth of Your servant David have said: 'Why did the nations rage, and the people plot vain things? The kings of the earth took their stand, and the rulers were gathered together against the Lord and against His Christ.'

"For truly against Your holy Servant Jesus, whom You anointed, both Herod and Pontius Pilate, with the Gentiles and the people of Israel, were gathered together to do whatever Your hand and Your purpose determined before to be done. *Now, Lord, look on their threats, and grant to Your servants that with all boldness they may speak Your word, by stretching out Your hand to heal, and that signs and wonders may be done through the name of Your holy Servant Jesus.*"

And when they had prayed, the place where they were assembled together was shaken; and they were all filled with the Holy Spirit, and they spoke the word of God with boldness.

—ACTS 4:21–31, EMPHASIS ADDED

This is spiritual warfare at its best! Their main request was for boldness to speak the Word of God without fear and that God would confirm His Word with the manifestation of signs and wonders.

God's Supernatural Response

The Scripture doesn't elaborate too much on what transpired after the early church prayed. As we just read, it simply states that "when they had prayed, the place where they were assembled together was shaken; and they were all filled with the Holy Spirit, and they spoke the word of God with boldness" (Acts 4:31). Two verses later the Scripture adds, "And with *great power* the apostles gave witness to the resurrection of the Lord Jesus. And *great grace* was upon them all (v. 33, emphasis added).

May God do it again! May He shake us and fill us with boldness! And may His great power and great grace rest upon the true church in this hour!

Four "Power Points" in the Early Church's Prayer

Let's look at four "power points" evident in the early church's prayer for boldness. There is much for us to learn from their example.

Power point #1

> Lord, You are God, who made heaven and earth and the sea, and all that is in them.
>
> —Acts 4:24

This opening statement recognizes several things:

+ **God's unlimited ability**—If He can make something as massive as the universe, He has the ability to bring anything in that universe into divine order.

+ **God's unlimited authority**—If He made the universe and all that is in it then He has the authority to change it.

+ **God's unlimited awareness**—Not only did God make a vast container (the universe), He made all that it contains (the detailed parts of creation). The

God of the macrocosm is the God of the micro-
cosm. He's not involved just in making extremely
large things; He's also involved in making extremely
small things. Both swirling galaxies and swirling
atoms occupy His attention. He is simultaneously
aware of both and upholds both with "the word of
His power" (Heb. 1:3).

God did not stop with creating only our physical forms;
He made each one of us a universe of thoughts, emotions,
gifts, abilities—and the individual compartments of God-
given potential are varied and many. The smallest areas of
need or potential in our lives are under His radar.

This statement in Acts 4:24 was also an acknowledge-
ment that the God of the Bible is absolute and supreme.
Many gods and goddesses were revered by the masses in that
Roman-infused era—and usually each deity was consigned
to a certain limited sphere of activity or authority. But the
true God is *Lord over all*!

Action step: *Remind God that He has supreme ability and authority,
that He can alter any circumstance, and that He is fully aware of
the most minute details of your circumstance.*

Power point #2

Who by the mouth of Your servant David have said: "Why
did the nations rage, and the people plot vain things? The
kings of the earth took their stand, and the rulers were
gathered together against the LORD and against His
Christ." For truly against Your holy Servant Jesus, whom
You anointed, both Herod and Pontius Pilate, with the
Gentiles and the people of Israel, were gathered together

to do whatever Your hand and Your purpose determined before to be done.

—ACTS 4:25–28

An important insight is revealed in these four verses. God foreknows all things and is not surprised or discouraged when opposition rises against His people. The apostles noted in this prayer that the Old Testament Scriptures actually foretold the rejection of the firstborn Son. Furthermore, while He was in the world, the Messiah Himself prophesied:

"A servant is not greater than his master." If they persecuted Me, they will also persecute you.

—JOHN 15:20

Just eight verses later He added:

These things I have spoken to you, that you should not be made to stumble [translated "should not be offended" in the KJV].

—JOHN 16:1

In other words, Jesus was assuring us that we will face rejection and we should not be surprised when it comes. In the midst of it all God's purpose will prevail for us. Even when people resist and reject the Word of the Lord, He is still on the throne.

Action step: *Remind God that nothing takes Him by surprise (He is omniscient). Declare that everything you face in life will end up furthering His purpose in you, that even in negative situations, He is still on the throne.*

Power point #3

> Now, Lord, look on their threats, and grant to Your ser-
> vants that with all boldness they may speak Your word.
> —Acts 4:29

The intercessors in the early church asked God to set His attention on what their enemies had said and done. Why? In order to thwart their intentions, counteract their strategies, and overcome their opposition by His superior wisdom and power. In a similar way we should ask God to set His attention on all the human and satanic strategies that have been forged against us—so that their efforts prove to be futile and powerless.

Those new covenant prayer warriors primarily petitioned God for boldness (aggressive courage in the face of opposition or challenge). Their hope was to declare the Word boldly. They knew God had done it before. David, the champion of Israel, even celebrated:

> In the day when I cried out, You answered me, and made
> me bold with strength in my soul.
> —Psalm 138:3

And Solomon, the proverb-writer, offered that:

> The righteous are bold as a lion.
> —Proverbs 28:1

One of the most intimidating aspects of a lion is its heart-seizing, mind-numbing roar. The other animals are gripped with fear when that sound rumbles through the jungle. So a bold church is one that "roars"—that unashamedly declares the truth, that fearlessly walks in faith and intimidates the opposition.

Lions are the king of wild beasts and will often boldly attack animals far larger in size. In the same way the church should not be afraid of tackling the largest problems: spiritually, socially, or politically.

Finally, lions are territorial. Every day they pace the perimeter of their claimed territory, leaving their scent to ward off any trespassers. So should we leave the scent of faith-filled worship as we boldly "pace around" the spiritual territory we have claimed for the kingdom of God.

Action step: *Ask God for boldness to speak His Word with lionlike fearlessness.*

Power point #4

> By stretching out Your hand to heal, and that signs and wonders may be done through the name of Your holy Servant Jesus.
>
> —Acts 4:30

Many scriptures refer to the "hand" of the Lord, such as:

+ "Behold, the Lord's hand is not shortened, that it cannot save" (Isa. 59:1).
+ "The right hand of the Lord is exalted; the right hand of the Lord does valiantly" (Ps. 118:16).
+ "The hand of the Lord shall be known to His servants, and His indignation to His enemies" (Isa. 66:14).

God promised the children of Israel that He would redeem them from Egypt's bondage with a "stretched-out arm" (Exod. 6:6). When something is stretched, it is extended beyond its ordinary limitations. So God was pledging to move for them in an exceptional way, far beyond the normal barrier between the supernatural and natural realms. So when the church prayed that God would stretch forth His hand, they were asking for the extraordinary to happen.

New covenant sons and daughters have been chosen to be a source of *signs and wonders* in the world. This is a major part of our calling, as prophesied in Isaiah 8:18 and confirmed in Hebrews 2:11–13.

Signs are exceptional supernatural happenings that are sent by God to confirm the Messiahship of Jesus, the truth of biblical doctrine, something God has said or someone He has anointed. Though we are not to seek signs for their own sake, the Bible promises that signs will follow us (Mark 16:16–18). God wants to give us signs if our hearts are right (Isa. 7:11).

Wonders are extraordinary supernatural happenings that awaken worshipful awe in the hearts of those who behold such divine intervention. Both signs and wonders are accomplished in the *name* of Jesus (by His authority and for His glory). To speak in His name is to speak as an oracle of God, as His representative, bearing His authority. He is still "Jesus of Nazareth, a man approved of God...by miracles and wonders and signs" (Acts 2:22, KJV). But now these signs and wonders are accomplished through His body on the earth.

Action step: *Ask God to stretch forth His hand and perform extraordinary signs and wonders by the authority of Jesus's name and for His glory.*

A Gang Leader Becomes a Soul Winner Overnight

In the beginning of my walk with the Lord I traveled with about five others in an old Volkswagen van, going from city to city witnessing on the streets. It was the early seventies, during the Jesus movement era, and God was doing amazing things. We constantly prayed for boldness (having read Acts chapter 4 many times), and we would deliberately put ourselves in situations where we had to manifest boldness and God had to manifest the supernatural if we were to survive. We expected signs and wonders to happen even on the street.

One of the most remarkable God encounters took place in Asheville, North Carolina. We were there to participate in a revival, and our custom was to hit the streets after church. One particular night after we prayed we went downtown. Encountering a police officer, we asked him to identify the worst area in the city. With a concerned look on his face, he responded, "Lexington Street—but don't go down there, preacher! You'll probably end up robbed and beat up. We'll find you crammed in a Dumpster with your throat slit." I calmly said, "Thank you, officer," and headed in the direction of Lexington Street, knowing in my heart of hearts that was the place that most needed our influence. As we started walking away, the officer just shook his head with an incredulous look on his face.[2]

When we arrived, we joined hands, bound the demonic forces, claimed the blessing of Joshua (that wherever we placed the soles of our feet, God would give us that territory), and prayed, "Your kingdom come; Your will be done," affirming God's dominion in that place. We split up and went different directions for about thirty minutes with little or no fruit resulting. Then it happened—the "portal of breakthrough" we always waited for.

A young man came crawling out of a dingy, raunchy

storefront bar, overdosing on a mixture of drugs and alcohol. Frothing at the mouth, convulsing, and barely able to crawl or to talk, he mumbled, "Preacher, pray for me." Apparently someone had told him a group of Christians were out on the street.

All of sudden the pure presence of God infiltrated the sensual, worldly atmosphere on that street. He just took over—radically—and He did it through us. Several of my team members gathered around this struggling soul and began casting out the devil that had him bound. Suddenly he looked up at us clear-eyed and exclaimed, "I'm not high! I'm not overdosing anymore. And I feel a strange power in the air all around me." I said, "That's the sweet Holy Spirit, and it feels even better when He comes on the inside." "I'm ready," he said. After I told him how to worship, he threw his hands up and started thanking God for filling him with the Holy Spirit.

About that time a young woman wearing only pink hot pants and a tiny halter top ran across the street and threw her arms around this newborn child of God. She kept gushing over and over, "Oh, I'm so happy for you; I'm so happy for you." I had no idea what was happening, but I knew God was orchestrating something. So I grabbed her hand and said, "Why don't you get what he just got?"

Without any more urging, she fell on her knees on a sidewalk littered with crushed beer cans and broken whiskey bottles and started praying and sobbing before God. I didn't find out until the next day that she had actually been raised in the Church of God, had been filled with the Spirit, and had sung in the choir. But she backslid during her teen years in a sad progression of parties, boys, cigarettes, beer, alcohol, and pills, until things got out of control. She finally found herself hooked on heroin and walking the streets as a prostitute to get the money for her next fix. As we prayed for this prodigal daughter, God soon moved mercifully in her life.

Then two winos stumbled up, dressed in tattered, vomit-covered clothing. They smelled terrible and looked as if they had slept too many nights huddled under an overpass. One of them pitifully pled with me, saying, "Could this Jesus who's helping them help us? We're just nobodies." I countered, "No, you're somebodies; you're the very reason Jesus came." I pulled them down into the prayer meeting that was intensifying with every passing moment. They quickly broke through into a real connection with God, weeping and accepting His salvation grace.

Then a backslidden Baptist preacher came up and informed us matter-of-factly, "I used to do what you people are doing. And I preached that if you ever had the goods, you would never fall from it. But I had a real relationship with God and, look, I lost it. It happened when everything went haywire in my life. My wife walked out on me and went into the world. Then my church turned against me, even though it wasn't my fault. One day I couldn't take it anymore. I drank just one beer, thinking it would calm my nerves, and I haven't stopped since. It's been two years now, and I've been drunk every day!" Tears began to flow down his cheeks as he said, "Now there are voices in my mind that tell me I'm reprobate and I'll never be able to get back to God."

Feeling a strong anointing gripping me, I defied that unbelief, shouting, "Those tears running down your face are the best sign to me that you're not reprobate. If you were, you'd be cursing me, not begging me to pray for you. Besides, the Bible says, 'The gifts and calling of God are without repentance.'" Then I grabbed his hand, and he fell into the prayer circle and started seeking God with the pent-up fervor of two years of anguish. Then something very unusual took place.

The young woman, set free and grateful, began singing "Amazing Grace." I have never experienced anything like it. It was as if her voice was amplified by the Holy Spirit, and it dominated the whole street. Then young man who was overdosing, the two winos, and the Baptist preacher all started singing with her. People started coming out of the bars to see what was going on. For a few minutes it looked as if we were going to start preaching to all of them, but then the person we should have been afraid of showed up, angry and ready for a confrontation.

A rugged and rough-looking man walked up who was well over six feet tall, built like a truck and seething with anger. He towered over me. We found out the next day he was a gang leader and the kingpin of criminal activity on the street, involved in drug dealing and a prostitution ring.

"What's going on here?" he bellowed.

"We're having a prayer meeting," I said.

"Nobody holds prayer meetings on Lexington Street."

"We do," I countered.

"How come?" he asked.

"Because we care about people," I explained.

He shot back, "Nobody cares about us; we're just a bunch of rejects!"

"We do!" I insisted.

Looking with unbelief, he said, "Who's in charge here anyway?"

"I am," I said, nodding my head.

Pointing down a long, dark, filthy alley, he spit out the words, "Come this way! I want to talk with you!" I gulped, thinking, "Now's as good a time as any to be a martyr."

When he got about fifty feet into the darkest part of the alley, he turned around, leaned over, got right in my face, and spoke through his teeth. I suppose he did all that to look and sound intimidating.

"Preacher, do you realize I left my house tonight intending to kill a man? If I had found him, I would have killed him."

Not wanting to rile him, I responded, "I guess you would have."

He leaned a little closer and said, "Do you realize I've got weapons in my pockets right now?"

As calmly as possible I replied, "I guess you do."

Finally, he growled, "You realize I could kill you right now if I wanted to?"

That's when the anointing rose up within me with boldness and I countered, "I guess you can't!"

Taken by surprise, he said, "And why not?"

I responded, "Because nothing's taking me out of this world until God's appointed time, and I happen to know it's not my time."

He broke into a weak smile and said, "Preacher, you've got guts. I was just testing you, anyway." (I felt so relieved.) Then he added, "I really brought you out here to ask you a question."

"What's that?" I asked, my face showing my relief.

"Your friends who came with you who were praying for

those drunks, I heard them speaking in strange languages. What was that?"

I said, "That's called speaking in tongues. It's a language of praise to God."

"That's strange," he said, "that's the way I hear my mama praying in a back room every time I go home."

My eyes got big with excitement. I busted out, "Your mama's prayers are about to be answered."

"What do mean?" he asked.

"You'll find out real soon," I told him.

That night we walked around Asheville talking about life and about the Bible until around 3 o'clock in the morning. That's when he said, "I'm ready, preacher," and he fell on his knees in a park, pouring his heart out to God. About ten minutes into our prayer time, he jumped up and ran away, saying, "I'll see you tomorrow night."

Little did I know, God had spoken to him that he needed to "clean house." He went home and woke up all the drunks, demanding that they pour their alcohol down the drain. Then he told the prostitutes they'd have to find another place to live and declared that from that day forward, his home was "God's house." You may already be shaking your head in amazement, but it gets even better.

The next night the converted gang leader busted through the swinging, western-style bar doors at the very bar where the revival outbreak happened the night before. He shouted in an overpowering way, "Shut the place down! Everybody's going to church tonight." Though protesting all the way, about ten of them followed him (a real motley crew), walking about two miles to our church. When the altar call was given that night, all looked at their new self-appointed "pastor." He motioned toward the altar, and they knew what he meant. They all went forward and repented.

What a stronghold of the power of darkness fell that night—and all because we prayed for boldness and dared to act when God poured it out! If I have ever witnessed a night of signs and wonders, that was it.

Oh, and by the way, six months later I went back to Asheville to find the gangster that I won to the Lord and learned that he had left town to go to Bible school and train to be a Church of God pastor. What better comment could I make to all these things than the opening line of the song that shook a city street, *"Amazing grace, how sweet the sound"*![3]

What About You?

Now it is time for you to pray, confess, and believe the power points in the prayer of the early church. The following bulleted statements summarize what we have learned in this chapter. After rehearsing these points, create your own prayer. Use as many parts of the early church prayer as you can. If at all possible, be sure to cover at least the four primary power points.

+ Declare that God is the sovereign Lord, ruler over the universe, and that all things were made by Him.

+ Declare God's omniscience and omnipotence, that He is all-knowing and all-powerful and that He knows every detail of your situation.

+ Announce that no negative thing in your life will ever take God by surprise, that He is well aware of any satanic strategies against you, and that He will cause all things to serve His eternal purpose.

+ Declare that God is on the throne, no matter what you face.

+ Ask God to fill you with boldness that you might represent Him with lionlike fearlessness and mastery.

+ Ask God to stretch forth His mighty hand on your behalf, just like He did when He carved a passageway through the impassable Red Sea.

+ Petition God to perform the miraculous—to manifest signs and wonders by the power of Jesus's name for His glory and the advance of His kingdom.

Now it's your turn to pray:

Lord God of Peter, James, John, and the early disciples, [compose your prayer as the Holy Spirit leads, drawing from the bullet points above].

Epilogue

PRAYERS THAT CHANGED THE WORLD FOREVER

B Y NOW YOU should feel the wind under your wings. By now you should have received a baptism of holy boldness, an awakening of consecrated confidence. We have the assurance that what God has done in the past, He can and will do again. He just needs vessels to work through. If He responded supernaturally to Moses, Solomon, Elijah, and the others featured in this book, we can expect Him to respond supernaturally to us.

I have often said, "The only thing unchangeable in this world is the God who said, 'I am the LORD; I change not' (Mal. 3:6, KJV)." Everything else is subject to change, especially when God's people pray in faith and the Almighty responds.

Don't minimize yourself. Elijah was a man who faced temptations and human frailties like the rest of us, but he walked in the supernatural. In fact, God was so appreciative of Elijah that when he finished his time in this world, God carried him supernaturally to heaven in a chariot of fire. How did he become such a history-maker and world-changer? The biblical explanation is, "He prayed" (James 5:17).

Other people in the past have prayed with such power that the world was changed forever, including the following key individuals.

Abel—Drawing Heaven to Earth

In the beginning, after the insurrection in Eden, spiritual darkness settled on the world like a thick, impenetrable fog— that is, until one man captured God's attention and drew His favor back into this realm. Adam and Eve had been exiled from the Garden of Eden. Their children had been born under the domination of Satan, the curse of death, and the horror of separation from God. Even though the "Presence of God" was apparently close by (see Gen. 4:16)—and at times He even spoke to them—hopelessness and despair must have surrounded the original family. But then Abel, the younger son, attempting to offer God true worship, presented a lamb without blemish as a burnt offering to God on an altar.

As far as we know, his was a wordless prayer, yet that sacrificed animal, consumed with fire, was a prophetic statement representing Abel's desire to present his life as a sacrifice to God and to be consumed with on-fire devotion to Him. The Most High honored his faith and "Abel…obtained witness that he was righteous, God testifying of his gifts" (Heb. 11:4).

What was this "witness"? We don't know for sure, but quite possibly supernatural fire fell from heaven and consumed Abel's sacrifice, since that happened later on when God found a sacrifice acceptable. (See Genesis 4:4–5, as well as 1 Kings 18:38, 2 Chronicles 7:1, and Leviticus 9:24.) Whatever took place, there must have been shrieks of terror among the evil principalities that thought they had erected an impassable barrier of satanic control in this fallen world. But God responded to Abel's prayer, the spiritual wall was breached, and a stream of blessing began flowing downward.

Like a barely burning ember coming back to life, renewed

hope started glowing in this world from that moment forward. Abel's testimony still echoes spiritually, and the flame still dances in the hearts of those who pray. Yes, "he being dead still speaks," urging the rest of us to seek God and expect a supernatural response that can change the unchangeable (Heb. 11:4). Things may look impossible for you now, but don't you think they looked even more impossible then? Yet one praying person made the difference.

Noah—Lifting a Curse

The story of this great patriarch's life is inarguably one of the most inspiring to be found in the Bible. After the flood was over, Noah's family and all the animals exited the ark.

> Then Noah built an altar to the LORD, and took of every clean animal and of every clean bird, and offered burnt offerings on the altar. And the LORD smelled a soothing aroma. Then the LORD said in His heart, "I will never again curse the ground for man's sake."
>
> —GENESIS 8:20–21

Another wordless prayer had profound global impact. It seems that up until that time it was almost impossible to grow any kind of substantial crop. Gripped with a suffocating curse, the ground primarily brought forth "thorns and thistles" (Gen. 3:18). Once again, though, a single individual touched the heart of God with his worship, and this time a debilitating curse was lifted from nature.

Prior to the flood, there had been only a mist rising up from the ground (Gen. 2:5–6). From that point forward, however, nourishing rain fell from above. After He saw Noah's reverential act, consecrating the new world, and He "smelled" the "soothing aroma" of passionate praise, the Most High God pledged: "While the earth remains, seedtime and harvest, cold and heat, winter and summer, and day and night shall not cease" (Gen. 8:22).

Was the flood caused by some catastrophe that resulted in the tilting of our axis twenty-three degrees, thus creating this seasonal pattern? Only God knows. All we can say for certain is the Creator chose at that time to communicate two vitally important things: (1) there would never be another flood and (2) the harvest cycle of nature would be recurring and predictable. Just because one man prayed. Most importantly, the curse originally pronounced on the entire earth was instead canceled—just because one man prayed.

Mary, Jesus's Mother—Releasing God's Will

The most monumental event ever to happen was the incarnation of the Son of God. Each major stage of His journey through time was activated by intercession. His first coming took place because many thousands of Jews had prayed for centuries that the Messiah would come. They longed to see the One who would fulfill the ancient prophecies:

+ The "Seed" of the woman destined to "bruise" the serpent's head (Gen. 3:15)

+ The "seed of Abraham" destined to bless all nations and families of the earth (Gen. 12:3; 22:18)

+ The "seed of David," who would cause his throne to endure forever (Ps. 89:29)

When the angel Gabriel announced that the ordained time had arrived, a humble Jewish girl prayerfully confessed:

"Behold the handmaid of the Lord; be it unto me according to thy word" (Luke 1:38, KJV).

That was a prayerful outburst, not only toward Gabriel but toward God Himself. The will of the Almighty was released, and nine months later, God became flesh, born of a virgin in a manger in Bethlehem. Jesus's life would prove to be the pivot on which the future of the world would turn. He was the holy One who came down to our level that He might lift us to His level. It was His plan from the beginning—yet it all hinged on a fourteen-word statement: the obedient, prayerful response of one common Jewish girl!

Jesus's Disciples—Interceding for Salvation

Approximately a third of a century later, at Jesus's triumphant entry into Jerusalem, His disciples jubilantly heralded the coming of the King of kings to the city of God, exclaiming:

> *Hosanna to the Son of David!* "Blessed is He who comes in the name of the LORD!" *Hosanna in the highest!*
> —Matthew 21:9, EMPHASIS ADDED

What faith-filled shouts of praise erupted from the crowd of enthusiastic worshippers that day! And what a moment for a unique worship word to surface in the Bible: *Hosanna*. You won't find it anywhere else, except, of course, in its original form in the Hebrew language.

You see, the New Testament word *Hosanna* actually evolved from a fusion of the traditional Hebrew praise words *hoshiah na*, which are a prayerful plea meaning, "Save now, I beseech You" (translated this way in Psalm 118:25 of the Modern King James Version). The Jewish worshippers that day understood this was a prophetic plea for the Messiah to set up His reign. However, even the apostles erroneously assumed this primarily meant deliverance from the oppressive Roman Empire. However, *much more* was effected than social and political freedom, for God is "able to do exceedingly abundantly above all that we ask or think" (Eph. 3:20).

Even though "Hosanna" is a prayerful request, strangely it is never spoken in a pleading tone of voice, as a petition. Instead, it is normally an ecstatic shout of praise. When I was first confronted with this paradox, I couldn't quite wrap my mind around it. So I brought up the subject to a dear Messianic Jewish friend, and he explained, "Oh, yes, *hoshiah na* is a request, but it is made in full expectation of performance. It is similar to a wife asking her husband, 'You will take out the garbage, won't you?' She may be 'asking,' but she has no doubt that her spouse will comply with her wishes and the action will take place."

And so it is with the beautiful praise word *Hosanna*. Technically it is an appeal, but it is spoken with an assurance of divine response. Though the strict translation is, "Save us, we beseech You," the implied meaning is "Lord, we fully believe You will save us and so we praise God for our deliverance in advance!"

When worshippers tag the phrase "in the highest" after the word *Hosanna*, it becomes an even more powerful proclamation. It is a potent way of declaring, "Lord, I believe You are going to save me in every area of my being *to the highest degree possible for God!*" How intense is that!

The phrase "Blessed is He who comes in the name of the LORD" was also understood to be a prophecy of the

Messiah—a declaration that He would represent the Father and be filled with His authority. The crowd of disciples waving palm fronds, casting their garments in the road, and shouting these words had no idea how profoundly their prayers would be answered in the next few days.

First Jesus "saved" them from corrupt religious profiteers, overturning the tables of the money changers. Then He was whipped in Pilate's hall, "saving" us all from the dominion of diseases and infirmities ("by whose stripes you were healed," 1 Pet. 2:24). Then He went to the cross to provide the salvation of our souls—conquering those archenemies of the human race: sin and Satan. Finally He descended into the "lower parts of the earth" to overcome death and hell, thus saving us to the "highest degree" possible (see Eph. 4:9–10).

So this worship phrase from an ancient text triggered the greatest spiritual upheaval ever to take place—and it sent a supernatural, seismic shudder through the whole planet with numerous aftershocks taking place all the way up to our day! Maybe that's why there were two earthquakes that notable week—one at the Crucifixion and another at the Resurrection. Everything was being shaken, and God caused the natural to reflect the spiritual!

Jesus—Praying for Spiritual Transformation

After Jesus ascended to heaven, He sent back the power of the Holy Spirit to His disciples on the Day of Pentecost. However, it is vital to see that even this grand infilling was the result of intercession—by the greatest intercessor of all, the Son of God Himself. Right before He collapsed in blood-sweating agony in the Garden of Gethsemane, He uttered the most powerful and pivotal petition ever to ascend to the Father of creation. It is found in John chapter 17.

Father…glorify Your Son, that Your Son also may glorify You, as You have given Him authority over all flesh, that He should give eternal life to as many as You have given Him. And this is eternal life, that they may know You, the only true God, and Jesus Christ whom You have sent.

I have manifested Your name to the men whom You have given Me out of the world. They were Yours, You gave them to Me, and they have kept Your word….For I have given to them the words which You have given Me; and they have received them….

Holy Father, keep through Your name those whom You have given Me, that they may be one as We are…that they may have My joy fulfilled in themselves….

I do not pray that You should take them out of the world, but that You should keep them from the evil one…Sanctify them by Your truth. Your word is truth….

I do not pray for these alone, but also for those who will believe in Me through their word; that they all may be one, as You, Father, are in Me, and I in You; that they also may be one in Us, that the world may believe that You sent Me. "And the glory which You gave Me I have given them, that they may be one just as We are one: I in them, and You in Me; that they may be made perfect in one, and that the world may know that You have sent Me, and have loved them as You have loved Me….

And I have declared to them Your name, and will declare it, that the love with which You loved Me may be in them, and I in them."

—John 17:1–26

How mightily the great High Priest stood in the gap for the disciples who would be waiting for the Holy Spirit in the Upper Room just over fifty days later! How powerfully that prayer has lingered ever since, hovering over the world in full potency for two millennia, released into manifestation each time a new convert receives the Lord Jesus into his heart.

Here are the main things for which Jesus prayed:

- That believers would receive the gift of eternal life
- That we would actually know God and receive the revelation of His name
- That we would receive and understand the Word of God
- That we would be kept from the evil one
- That we would be sanctified (cleansed from the defilement of sin and consecrated to God)
- That we would be accepted into the same oneness with the Father that Jesus enjoyed
- That we would be brought to perfection
- That the love of the Father would abide within us
- That the Son of God would live within us

What an awe-inspiring event it was when that first group of believers received the fruit of this intercession. The "Helper" (the Holy Spirit) came into the Upper Room like "a rushing mighty wind," and divided "tongues of fire" hovered over them (Acts 2:2–3). Surely that "wind" was the very breath of God breathing into His people the restoration of what Adam lost in the garden.

The supernatural transformation forecast in this prayer

has been only partially implemented but will be brought to complete fulfillment in the not-so-distant future when the "dead in Christ" rise and the "living believers" are caught up with them to meet the Lord in the air at His Second Coming. (See 1 Thessalonians 4:16–17.) We will then be made *utterly perfect*: changed and glorified in a moment, in the twinkling of an eye, when the King of kings comes "in His glory, and all the holy angels with Him" (Matt. 25:31). We will then be so filled with His magnificence that we will shine "like the sun in the kingdom" of our Father (Matt. 13:43).

The Prayer of the Church—for the Kingdom and the King to Come in Full Manifestation

When the Lord returns, the prayer Jesus told His followers to pray will be finally, gloriously fulfilled:

> Our Father in heaven, hallowed be Your name. *Your kingdom come. Your will be done on earth as it is in heaven.*
> —Matthew 6:9–10, emphasis added

Millions of believing voices have uttered these prophetic words tens of millions of times through the past twenty centuries—and not in vain. Though the kingdom of God came into the world spiritually on the Day of Pentecost, it will merge completely with the natural world when the Lord of hosts rends the heavens and comes down. Evil will be banished. Satan will be bound in a bottomless pit. The love of God that surpasses knowledge will abound. Joy unspeakable and peace that surpasses all understanding will drive all darkness from the planet. At that time:

Nation shall not lift up sword against nation, neither shall they learn war anymore.

—Micah 4:3

"The wolf and the lamb shall feed together, the lion shall eat straw like the ox....They shall not hurt nor destroy in all My holy mountain," says the Lord.

—Isaiah 65:25

For the earth will be filled with the knowledge of the glory of the Lord, as the waters cover the sea.

—Habakkuk 2:14

So you see, you are already doing it—you and around two billion other believers currently in this world. Every time you petition the "blessed and only Potentate" with the inspired words, "Your kingdom come; Your will be done," you are praying a prayer that will inevitably *change the world forever.* Every time you plead, *"Father...deliver us from evil,"* God's answer extends far beyond your own personal life to ultimately encircle the entire globe with His deliverance power.

Maybe you thought that kind of prayer power was reserved for the recognized champions of the faith, but God loves to use common people to accomplish uncommon things.

Yes, of all the prayerful utterances that have been uttered in this world, this "powerful prayer" really will produce "supernatural results." And it will absolutely be answered—gloriously and permanently—in a moment.

It is no wonder that the "Spirit and the bride say, 'Come!'" (Rev. 22:17). Because just one prayerful statement—"Come"—sent upward to the enthroned Messiah has incredible power when spoken with faith and love.

Go ahead. Gaze up to the highest heaven and pray, "Come,

Lord Jesus!" The inevitable, prophesied response from on high will be so spectacular, so glorious, so transformational that no human words can sufficiently describe it.

Surely Isaiah's heart was pumping hard with spiritual adrenaline when he saw and declared the ultimate outcome:

> Moreover the light of the moon will be as the light of the sun, and the light of the sun will be sevenfold, as the light of seven days, in the day that the Lord binds up the bruise of His people and heals the stroke of their wound.
> —Isaiah 30:26

After many centuries of petitions ascending to heaven, the answer will come in one blinding flash of power. Your prayers and the prayers of the rest of the body of Christ, like burning incense swirling around the very throne of the Almighty, will soon attract an incomparable response from on high (Rev. 8:1–6).

When that happens, Jesus will descend in flaming fire accompanied by all His holy angels. Every eye will see Him, the dead in Christ will rise, living believers will be translated, the kingdom will fully come to earth—and the world will finally be changed forever.

So, child of God, "pray for the peace of Jerusalem" in an ultimate and absolute sense (Ps. 122:6). Pray that the Prince of peace will be enthroned there and His peace like a river will fill the earth. If that can happen (in such a divided, war-torn part of the world), then anything can happen when God's people pray.

Don't ever give up. Keep seeking His face.

Supernatural results are awaiting.

NOTES

Introduction

1. Ron Rhodes, *1001 Unforgettable Quotes About God Faith and the Bible* (Eugene, OR: Harvest House Publishers, 2011), 168.

2. As quoted in Sue Curran, *Define Your Destiny Through Prayer* (Shippensburg, PA: Destiny Image, 2012).

Chapter 1—The Prayer of Moses

1. Oswald Chambers, "My Utmost for His Highest," October 17, 2013, http://utmost.org/the-key-of-the-greater-work/ (accessed June 27, 2014); David Jeremiah, *Prayer, the Great Adventure* (Orange, CA: Multnomah Books, 2010).

2. As quoted in Cheri Fuller, *A Busy Woman's Guide to Prayer* (Brentwood, TN: Integrity Publishers, 2005), 50.

Chapter 4—The Prayer of Solomon #2

1. G. W. Bromiley, *The International Standard Bible Encyclopedia*, (Grand Rapids, MI: Eerdmans, 1986).

2. As quoted in Wendy Griffith and Craig Von Buseck, *Praying the News* (Ventura, CA; Regal, 2011).

Chapter 5—The Prayer of Asa

1. As quoted in Mary Ann Bridgwater and Beth Moore, *Prayers for the Faithful* (Nashville, TN: B&H Publishing Group 2008).

2. As quoted in Victor Parachin, *Daily Strength for Daily Needs* (Liguori, MO: Liguori, 1998).

Chapter 6—The Prayer of Jehoshaphat

1. Roswell D. Hitchcock, *Hitchcock's Bible Names Dictionary* (Oxford: Benediction Classics, 2010).

2. As quoted in Herbert Lockyer, *All the Promises of the Bible* (Grand Rapids, MI: Zondervan, 1962), 10.

Chapter 8—The Prayer of Jonah

1. William Smith, *Smith's Bible Dictionary* (Westwood, NJ: Barbour, 1987).

2. To read other commentaries discussing Jonah's drowning and/or descent into hell, see Ethelbert William Bullinger, "Commentary on Jonah 1:1," *E. W. Bullinger's Companion Bible Notes*," 1909–1922, http://www.studylight.org/commentaries/bul/view.cgi?bk=jon&ch=1 (accessed August 25, 2014); *The Dake Annotated Reference Bible* (Lawrenceville, GA: Dake Publishing, 1996), footnote for Jonah 2:2, which says Jonah prayed "from both places—the belly of the fish, and hell; for he was in both places, his soul being in hell between the time of his death and resurrection"; and Herbert Lockyer, *All the Miracles of the Bible* (Grand Rapids, MI: Zondervan, 1961), 144–145, which says: "Personally, we believe that the miraculous in this transaction was not in Jonah's preservation alive and conscious for three days and three nights in a living prison, but in his resurrection after having died….A comparison of Matthew 12:40; 16:4 with 1 Corinthians 15:4 shows that the period of Jonah's stay in the fish was divinely ordered to be a type of Christ's being 'three days and three nights in the heart of the earth.' In both cases we affirm there was death and resurrection…Further, Jonah prayed 'out of the belly of hell' (2:2) and the basic meaning of the word 'hell' is sheol, the sphere of departed bodies."

3. Dictionary.com, s.v. "think," http://dictionary.reference.com/browse/think (accessed July 11, 2014).

Chapter 9—The Prayer of Hezekiah

1. Hitchcock, *Hitchcock's Bible Names Dictionary*.

Chapter 10—The Prayer of the Early Church

1. Christian Quotes, "F. B. Meyer on Prayer," http://christian-quotes .ochristian.com/christian-quotes_ochristian.cgi?find=Christian-quotes -by-F.B.+Meyer-on-Prayer (accessed July 11, 2014).

2. It should be noted that the city of Asheville, North Carolina, has greatly upgraded this part of their city so that now it is a very pleasant and interesting area to visit.

3. "Amazing Grace" by John Newton. Public domain.

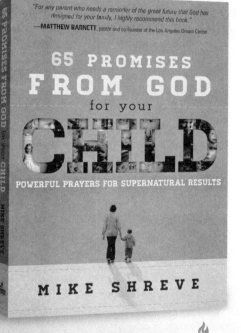